BOOKS AND PERSONS

ARNOLD BENNETT

BY ARNOLD BENNETT

NOVELS

THE LION'S SHARE
THESE TWAIN
CLAYHANGER
HILDA LESSWAYS
THE OLD WIVES' TALE
DENRY THE AUDACIOUS
THE OLD ADAM
HELEN WITH THE HIGH HAND
THE MATADOR OF THE FIVE TOWNS
THE BOOK OF CARLOTTA
BURIED ALIVE
A GREAT MAN
LEONORA
WHOM GOD HATH JOINED
A MAN FROM THE NORTH
ANNA OF THE FIVE TOWNS
THE GLIMPSE
THE CITY OF PLEASURE
THE GRAND BABYLON HOTEL
HUGO
THE GATES OF WRATH

POCKET PHILOSOPHIES

THE AUTHOR'S CRAFT
MARRIED LIFE
FRIENDSHIP AND HAPPINESS
HOW TO LIVE ON 24 HOURS A DAY
THE HUMAN MACHINE
LITERARY TASTE
MENTAL EFFICIENCY

PLAYS

THE GREAT ADVENTURE
CUPID AND COMMONSENSE
WHAT THE PUBLIC WANTS
POLITE FARCES
THE HONEYMOON

IN COLLABORATION WITH EDWARD KNOBLAUCH
MILESTONES

MISCELLANEOUS

BOOKS AND PERSONS
PARIS NIGHTS
THE TRUTH ABOUT AN AUTHOR
LIBERTY
OVER THERE: WAR SCENES

NEW YORK: GEORGE H. DORAN COMPANY

Books and Persons

BEING COMMENTS ON A
PAST EPOCH

1908-1911

BY
ARNOLD BENNETT

NEW YORK
George H. Doran Company

PRINTED IN THE UNITED STATES OF AMERICA

TO

HUGH WALPOLE

PREFATORY NOTE

THE contents of this book have been chosen from a series of weekly articles which enlivened the *New Age* during the years 1908, 1909, 1910, and 1911, under the pseudonym "Jacob Tonson." The man responsible for the republication is the dedicatee, who, having mysteriously demanded from me back numbers of the *New Age*, sat in my house one Sunday afternoon and in four hours read through the entire series. He then announced that he had made a judicious selection, and that the selection must positively be issued in volume form. Mr. Frank Swinnerton approved the selection and added to it slightly. In my turn I suggested a few more additions. The total amounts to one-third of the original matter. Beyond correcting misprints, softening the crudity of several epithets, and censoring lines here and there which might give offence without helping the sacred cause, I have not altered the articles. They appear as they were journalistically written in Paris, London, Switzerland, and the Forest of

Fontainebleau. In particular I have left the critical judgments alone, for the good reason that I stand by nearly all of them, though perhaps with a less challenging vivacity, to this day.

ARNOLD BENNETT

February, 1917

CONTENTS

1908

CONTENTS

1909

CONTENTS

CONTENTS

1908

WILFRED WHITTEN'S PROSE

AN important book on an important town *4 Apr. '08* is to be issued by Messrs. Methuen. The town is London, and the author Mr. Wilfred Whitten, known to journalism as John o' London. Considering that he comes from Newcastle-on-Tyne (or thereabouts, his pseudonym seems to stretch a point. However, Mr. Whitten is now acknowledged as one of the foremost experts in London topography. He is not an archæologist, he is a humanist—in a good dry sense; not the University sense, nor the silly sense. The word "human" is a dangerous word; I am rather inclined to handle it with antiseptic precautions. When a critic who has risen high enough to be allowed to sign his reviews in a daily paper calls a new book "a great human novel," you may be absolutely sure that the said novel consists chiefly of ridiculous twaddle. Mr. Whitten is not a humanist in that sense. He has no sentimentality, and a very great deal of both wit and humour.

He is also a critic admirably sane. Not long ago he gave a highly diverting exhibition of sanity in a short, shattering pronounce-

4 Apr. '08 ment upon the works of Mr. Arthur Christopher Benson and the school which has acquired celebrity by holding the mirror up to its own nature. The wonder was that Mr. Benson did not, following his precedent, write to the papers to say that Mr. Whitten was no gentleman. In the days before the *Academy* blended the characteristics of a comic paper with those of a journal of dogmatic theology, before it took to disowning its own reviewers, Mr. Whitten was the solid foundation of that paper's staff. He furnished the substance, which was embroidered by the dark grace of the personality of Mr. Lewis Hind, whose new volume of divagations is, by the way, just out.

But my main object in referring to Mr. Whitten is to state formally, and with a due sense of responsibility, that he is one of the finest prose writers now writing in English. His name is on the title-pages of several books, but no book of his will yet bear out my statement. The proof of it lies in weekly papers. No living Englishman can do "the grand manner"—combining majestic dignity with a genuine lyrical inspiration—better than Mr. Whitten. These are proud words of mine, but I am not going to disguise my conviction that I know what I am talking about. Some day some publisher will wake up out of the coma in which publishers exist, and publish in volume form—probably with coloured pictures as jam for children—Mr. Whitten's descriptions of English towns. Then I shall be justified. I might have waited till that august moment. But I want to be beforehand with Dr. Robertson Nicoll. I see that Dr. Robertson Nicoll has just added to his list of patents by inventing Leonard Merrick, whom I used to admire in print long before Dr. Nicoll had ever heard that Mr. J. M. Barrie regarded Leonard Merrick as the foremost English novelist. Dr. Nicoll has already got Mr. Whitten on to the reviewing staff of the *Bookman*. But I am determined that he shall not invent Mr. Whitten's prose style. I am the inventor of that. *4 Apr. '08*

A few weeks ago I claimed to be the discoverer of Mr. Wilfred Whitten as a first-class prose writer. I relinquished the claim with apologies. Messrs. Methuen have staggered me by sending me Mrs. Laurence Binyon's *Nineteenth Century Prose*, in which anthology is an example of Mr. Whitten's prose. Though staggered, I was delighted. *2 May '08*

2 May '08 I should very much like to know how Mrs. Binyon encountered the prose of Mr. Whitten. Did she hunt through the files of newspapers for what she might find therein, and was she thus rewarded? Or did some tremendous and omniscient expert give her the tip? I disagree with about 85 per cent. of the obiter dicta of her preface, but her anthology is certainly a most agreeable compilation. It shows, like sundry other recent anthologies, the strong liberating influence of Mr. E. V. Lucas, whose "Open Road" really amounted to a renascence of the craft.

And here is the tail-end of the extract which Mrs. Binyon has perfectly chosen from the essays of Mr. Whitten:

". . . The moon pushing her way upwards through the vapours, and the scent of the beans and kitchen stuff from the allotments, and the gleaming rails below, spoke of the resumption of daily burdens. But let us drop that jargon. Why call that a burden which can never be lifted? This calm necessity that dwells with the matured man to get back to the matter in hand, and dree his weird whatever befall, is a badge, not a burden. It is the stimulus of sound natures; and as the weight of his wife's arm makes a man's body proud, so the sense of his usefulness to the world does but warm and indurate his soul. It is something when a man comes to this mind, and with all his capacity to err, is abreast of life at last. He shall not regret the infrequency of his inspirations, for he will know that the day of his strength has set in. And if, for poesy, some grave Virgilian line should pause on his memory, or some tongue of Hebrew fire leap from the ashes of his godly youth, it will be enough. But if cold duck await—why, then, to supper!" *2 May '08*

UGLINESS IN FICTION

9 May '08 IN the *Edinburgh Review* there is a disquisition on "Ugliness in Fiction." Probably the author of it has read "Liza of Lambeth," and said Faugh! The article, peculiarly inept, is one of those outpourings which every generation of artists has to suffer with what tranquillity it can. According to the Reviewer, ugliness is specially rife "just now." It is always "just now." It was "just now" when George Eliot wrote "Adam Bede," when George Moore wrote "A Mummer's Wife," when Thomas Hardy wrote "Jude the Obscure." As sure as ever a novelist endeavours to paint a complete picture of life in this honest, hypocritical country of bad restaurants and good women; as sure as ever he hints that all is not for the best in the best of all possible islands, some witling is bound to come forward and point out with wise finger that life is not all black. I once resided near a young noodle of a Methodist pastor who had the pious habit of reading novels aloud to his father and mother. He began to read one of mine to them, but half-way through decided that something of Charlotte M. Yonge would be less unsuitable for the parental ear. He then called and lectured me. Among other aphorisms of his which I have treasured up was this: "Life, my dear friend, is like an April day—sunshine and shadow chasing each other over the plain." That he is not dead is a great tribute to my singular self-control. I suspect him to be the Edinburgh Reviewer. At any rate, the article moves on the plane of his plain. *9 May '08*

The Reviewer has the strange effrontery to select Mr. Joseph Conrad's "Secret Agent" as an example of modern ugliness in fiction: a novel that is simply steeped in the finest beauty from end to end. I do not suppose that the *Edinburgh Review* has any moulding influence upon the evolution of the art of fiction in this country. But such nonsense may, after all, do harm by confusing the minds of people who really are anxious to encourage what is best, strongest, and most sane. The Reviewer in this instance, for example, classes, as serious, Thomas Hardy, Joseph Conrad, and John Galsworthy, who are genuine creative forces, with mere dignified unimportant sentimentalisers like Mr. W. B. Maxwell. While he was on the business of sifting the serious from the unserious I wonder he didn't in-

9 May '08 clude the authors of "Three Weeks" and "The Heart of a Child" among the serious! Perhaps because the latter wrote "Pigs in Clover," and the former was condemned by the booksellers! Nobody could have a lower opinion of "Three Weeks" than I have. But I have never been able to understand why the poor little feeble story was singled out as an awful example of female licentiousness, and condemned by a hundred newspapers that had not the courage to name it. The thing was merely infantile and absurd. Moreover, I violently object to booksellers sitting in judgment on novels.

LETTERS OF QUEEN VICTORIA

THE result of Murray v. the *Times* is very amusing. I don't know why the fact that the *Times* is called upon to pay £7500 to Mr. John Murray should make me laugh joyously; but it does. Certainly the reason is not that I sympathize with the libelled Mr. Murray. The action was a great and a wonderful action, full of enigmas for a mere man of letters like myself. For example, Mr. Murray said that his agreement with the "authors" (I cannot imagine how Lord Esher and Mr. A. C. Benson came to be the "authors" of the late Queen's correspondence) stipulated that two-thirds of the profits should go to the "authors" and one-third to Mr. Murray. Secondly, Mr. Murray said that he paid the authors £5592 14s. 2d. Thirdly, he said that his own profit was £600. Hence £600 is the half of £5592 14s. 2d. I have no doubt that there exists some quite simple explanation of this new arithmetic; only it has not occurred to me, my name not being Colenso. The whole enterprise was regal, as befitted. Proof-corrections cost twice as much as the original setting up! A mere man of letters would be inclined to suspect that the printing was begun *16 May '08*

16 May '08 too soon; it is usual to postpone setting-up a book until the book is written. Balzac partially beggared himself by ignoring this rule. Balzac, however, was not published by Mr. Murray. £950 was paid to the amanuensis! Oh, amanuensis, how I wonder who you are, up above the world so high, like a fashionable novelist in the sky! And so on.

The attitude of Tunbridge Wells (the most plutocratic town in England, by the way) towards the book was adorable. "Mr. Daniel Williams, a bookseller and librarian, of Tunbridge Wells, said that after the review by 'Artifex' people complained that the price of the book was too high. No complaints were made before that." They read their *Times Literary Supplement* at the Wells, and they still wait for it to thunder, and when it has thundered—and not before—they rattle their tea-trays, and the sequel is red ruin! Again, Mr. Justice Darling, in his ineptly decorated summing-up, observed that it was hardly too much to say that "the plaintiff's house—the house of Murray," was a national institution. It would be hardly too much to say that also the house of Crosse and Blackwell is a national institution, and that Mr. Justice Darling is a national institution. By all means let us count the brothers Murray as a national institution, even as an Imperial institution. But let us guard against the notion, everywhere cropping up, that such "houses" as the dignified and wealthy house of Murray are in some mysterious way responsible for English literature, part-authors of English literature, to whom half of the glory of English literature is due. It is well to remember now and then that publishers who have quite squarely made vast sums out of selling the work of creative artists are not thereby creative artists themselves. A publisher is a tradesman; infinitely less an artist than a tailor is an artist. Often a publisher knows what the public will buy in literature. Very rarely he knows what is good literature. Scarcely ever will he issue a distinguished book exclusively because it is a distinguished book. And he is right, for he is only a tradesman. But to judge from the otiose majesty of some publishers, one would imagine that they had written at least "Childe Harold." There is the case of a living publisher (not either of the brothers Murray) whose presence at his country château is indicated to the surrounding nobility, gentry, and peasantry by the *16 May '08*

16 May '08 unfurling of the Royal standard over a turret.

❦

To return to the subject, the price at which the house of Murray issued the "Letters of Queen Victoria" was not "extortionate," having regard to the astounding expenses of publication. But why were the expenses so astounding? If the book had not been one which by its intrinsic interest compelled purchase, would the "authors" have been remunerated like the managers of a steel trust? Would the paper have been so precious and costly? Would the illustrations have so enriched photographers? And would the amanuensis have made £350 more out of the thing than Mr. Murray himself? The price was not extortionate. But it was farcical. The entire rigmarole combines to throw into dazzling prominence the fact that modern literature in this country is still absolutely undemocratic. The time will come, and much sooner than many august mandarins anticipate, when such a book as the "Letters of Queen Victoria" will be issued at six shillings, and newspapers will be fined £7500 for saying that the price is extortionate and ought not to exceed half-a-crown. Assuredly there is no commercial reason why the book should not have been published at 6s. or thereabouts. Only mandarinism prevented that. Mr. Murray's profits would have been greater, though "authors," amanuenses, photographers, paper-makers, West-End booksellers, and other parasitic artisans might have suffered slightly. *16 May '08*

FRENCH PUBLISHERS

23 May '08 It has commonly been supposed that the publication of Flaubert's "Madame Bovary" resulted, at first, in a loss to the author. I am sure that everyone will be extremely relieved to learn, from a letter recently printed in "L'Intermédiaire" (the French equivalent of "Notes and Queries"), that the supposition is incorrect. Here is a translation of part of the letter, written by the celebrated publishers, Poulet-Malassis, to an author unnamed. The whole letter is very interesting, and it would probably reconcile the "author" of the correspondence of Queen Victoria to the sweating system by which they received the miserable sum of £5592 14s. 2d. from Mr. John Murray for their Titanic labours.

23 October, 1857.

"I think, sir, that you are in error as to Messrs. Lévy's method of doing business. Messrs. Lévy buy for 400 francs [£16] the right to publish a book during four years. It was on these terms that they bought the stories of Jules de la Madeleine, Flaubert's "Madame Bovary," etc. These facts are within my knowledge. To take an example among translations, they bought from Baudelaire, for 400 francs, the right to publish 6,000 copies of his Poé. We do not work in this way. We buy for 200 francs (£8) the right to publish an edition of 1,200 copies. . . . If the book succeeds, so much the better for the author, who makes 200 francs out of every edition of 1,200 copies. If M. Flaubert, whose book is in its third edition, had come to us instead of to Messrs. Lévy, his book would already have brought him in 1,000 francs (£40); during the four years that Messrs. Lévy will have the rights of his book for a total payment of 400 francs, he might have made two or three thousand francs with us. . . . Votre vien dévoué, A. P. Malassis. *23 May '08*

We now know that Flaubert made £16 in four years out of "Madame Bovary," which went into three editions within considerably less than a year of publication. And yet the house of Lévy is one of the most respectable and grandoise in France. Moral: English authors ought to go down on their knees and thank God that English publishers are not as other publishers. At least, not always!

WORDSWORTH'S SINGLE LINES

30 May '08 I HAVE had great joy in Mr. Nowell Charles Smith's new and comprehensive edition of Wordsworth, published by Methuen in three volumes as majestic as Wordsworth himself at his most pontifical. The price is fifteen shillings net, and having regard to the immense labour involved in such an edition, it is very cheap. I would sooner pay fifteen shillings for a real book like this than a guinea for the memories of any tin god that ever sat up at nights to keep a diary; yea, even though the average collection of memoirs will furnish material to light seven hundred pipes. We have lately been much favoured with first-rate editions of poets. I mention Mr. de Sélincourt's Keats, and Mr. George Sampson's amazing and not-to-be-sufficiently-lauded Blake. Mr. Smith's work is worthy to stand on the same shelf with these. A shining virtue of Mr. Smith's edition is that it embodies the main results of the researches and excavations not only of Professor Knight, but, more important, of the wonderful Mr. Hutchinson, whose contributions to the

Academy, in days of yore, were the delight of Wordsworthians. *30 May '08*

Personally, I became a member of the order of Wordsworthians in the historic year 1891, when Matthew Arnold's "Selections" were issued to the public at the price of half-a-crown. I suppose that Matthew Arnold and Sir Leslie Stephen were the two sanest Wordsworthians of us all. And Matthew Arnold put Wordsworth above all modern poets except Dante, Shakespeare, Goethe, Milton, and Molière. The test of a Wordsworthian is the ability to read with pleasure every line that the poet wrote. I regret to say that, strictly, Matthew Arnold was not a perfect Wordsworthian; he confessed, with manly sincerity, that he could not read "Vaudracour and Julia" with pleasure. This was a pity and Matthew Arnold's loss. For a strict Wordsworthian, while utterly conserving his reverence for the most poetic of poets, can discover a keen ecstasy in the perusal of the unconsciously funny lines which Wordsworth was constantly perpetrating. And I would back myself to win the first prize in any competition for Wordsworth's funniest line with a quotation from

30 May '08 "Vaudracour and Julia." My prize-line would assuredly be:

> *Yea, his first word of greeting was,—*
> *"All right . . .*

It is true that the passage goes on:

> *Is gone from me. . . .*

But that does not impair the magnificent funniness.

From his tenderest years Wordsworth succeeded in combining the virtues of Milton and of *Punch* in a manner that no other poet has approached. Thus, at the age of eighteen, he could write:

> *Now while the solemn evening shadows sail,*
> *On slowly-waving pinions, down the vale;*
> *And fronting the bright west, yon oak entwines*
> *Its darkening boughs. . . .*

Which really is rather splendid for a boy. And he could immediately follow that, speaking of a family of swans, with:

> *While tender cares and mild domestic loves*
> *With furtive watch pursue her as she moves,*
> *The female with a meeker charm succeeds. . .*

WORDSWORTH'S SINGLE LINES

Wordsworth richly atoned for his unconscious farcicalness by a multitude of single lines that, in their pregnant sublimity, attend the Wordsworthian like a shadow throughout his life, warning him continually when he is in danger of making a fool of himself. Thus, whenever through mere idleness I begin to waste the irrecoverable moments of eternity, I always think of that masterly phrase (from, I think, the "Prelude," but I will not be sure): *30 May '08*

Unprofitably travelling towards the grave.

This line is a most convenient and effective stone to throw at one's languid friends. Finally let me hail Mr. Nowell Smith as a benefactor.

NOVELISTS AND AGENTS

20 June '08 A BAD publishing season is now drawing to a close, and in the air are rumours of a crisis. Of course the fault is the author's. It goes without saying that the fault is the author's. In the first place, he will insist on producing mediocre novels. (For naturally the author is a novelist; only novelists count when crises loom. Algernon Charles Swinburne, Edward Carpenter, Robert Bridges, Lord Morley—these types have no relation to crises.) It appears that the publishers have been losing money over the six-shilling novel, and that they are not going to stand the loss any longer. It is stated that never in history were novels so atrociously mediocre as they are to-day. And in the second place, the author will insist on employing an Unspeakable Rascal entitled a literary agent, and the poor innocent lamb of a publisher is fleeced to the naked skin by this scoundrel every time the two meet. Already I have heard that one publisher, hitherto accustomed to the services of twenty gardeners at his country house, has been obliged to reduce the horticultural staff to eighteen.

Such is the publishers' explanation of the crisis. I shall keep my own explanation till the crisis is a little more advanced and ready to burst. In the meantime I should like to ask: How *do* people manage to range over the whole period of the novel's history and definitely decide that novels were never so bad as they are now? I am personally inclined to think that at no time has the average novel been so good as it is to-day. (This view, by the way, is borne out by publishers' own advertisements, which abound in the word "masterpiece" quoted from infallible critics of great masterpieces!) Let any man who disagrees with me dare go to Mudie's and get out a few forgotten novels of thirty years ago and try to read them! Also, I am prepared to offer £50 for the name and address of a literary agent who is capable of getting the better of a publisher. I am widely acquainted with publishers and literary agents, and though I have often met publishers who have got the better of literary agents, I have never met a literary agent who has come out on top of a publisher. Such a literary agent is badly wanted. I have been looking for him for years. I know a number of authors who would join me in enriching that literary *20 June '08*

20 June '08 agent. The publishers are always talking about him. I seldom go into a publisher's office but that literary agent has just left (gorged with illicit gold). It irritates me that I cannot run across him. If I were a publisher, he would have been in prison ere now. Briefly, the manner in which certain prominent publishers, even clever ones, talk about literary agents is silly.

Still, I am ready to believe that publishers have lost money over the six-shilling novel. I am acquainted with the details of several instances of such loss. And in every case the loss has been the result of gambling on the part of the publisher. I do not hesitate to say that the terms offered in late years by some publishers to some popular favourites have been grotesquely inflated. Publishers compete among themselves, and then, when the moment comes for paying the gambler's penalty, they complain of having been swindled. Note that the losses of publishers are nearly always on the works of the idols of the crowd. They want the idol's name as an ornament to their lists, and they commit indiscretions in order to get it. Fantastic terms are never offered to the solid, regular, industrious medium novelist. And it is a surety that fantastic terms are never offered to the beginner. Ask, and learn. *20 June '08*

But though I admit that money has been lost, I do not think the losses have been heavy. After all, no idolized author and no diabolic agent can force a publisher to pay more than he really wants to pay. And no diabolic agent, having once bitten a publisher, can persuade that publisher to hold out his generous hand to be bitten again. These are truisms. Lastly, I am quite sure that, out of books, a great deal more money has been made by publishers than by authors, and that this will always be so. The threatened crisis in publishing has nothing to do with the prices paid to authors, which on the whole are now fairly just (very different from what they were twenty years ago, when authors had to accept whatever was condescendingly offered to them). And if a crisis does come, the people to suffer will happily be those who can best afford to suffer.

THE NOVEL OF THE SEASON

11 July '08

THE publishing season—the bad publishing season—is now practically over, and publishers may go away for their holidays comforted by the fact that they will not begin to lose money again till the autumn. It only remains to be decided which is the novel of the season. Those interested in the question may expect it to be decided at any moment, either in the *British Weekly* or the *Sphere.* I take up these journals with a thrill of anticipation. For my part, I am determined only to decide which is not the novel of the season. There are several novels which are not the novel of the season. Perhaps the chief of them is Mr. E. C. Booth's "The Cliff End," which counts among sundry successes to the score of Mr. Grant Richards. Everything has been done for it that reviewing can do, and it has sold, and it is an ingenious and giggling work, but not the novel of the season.

The reviews of "The Cliff End," almost unanimously laudatory, show in a bright light our national indifference to composition in art. Some reviewers, while stating that the story itself was a poor one, insisted that

THE NOVEL OF THE SEASON

11 July '08

Mr. Booth is a born and accomplished story-teller. Story-tellers born and accomplished do not tell poor stories. A poor story is the work of a poor story-teller. And the story of "The Cliff End" is merely absurd. It is worse, if possible, than the story of Mr. Maxwell's "Vivien," which reviewers accepted. It would appear that with certain novels the story doesn't matter! I really believe that composition, the foundation of all arts, including the art of fiction, is utterly unconsidered in England. Or if it is considered, it is painfully misunderstood. I remember how the panjandrums condescendingly pointed out the bad construction of Mr. Joseph Conrad's "Lord Jim," one of the most noble examples of fine composition in modern literature, and but slightly disfigured by a detail of clumsy machinery. In "The Cliff End" there is simply no composition that is not clumsy and conventional. All that can be said of it is that you can't read a page, up to about page 200, without grinning. (Unhappily Mr. Booth overestimated his stock of grins, which ran out untimely.) The true art of fiction, however, is not chiefly connected with grinning, or with weeping. It consists, first and mainly, in a beautiful general composition.

11 July '08 But in Anglo-Saxon countries any writer who can induce both a grin and a tear on the same page, no matter how insolent his contempt for composition, is sure of that immortality which contemporaries can award.

Another novel that is not the novel of the season is Mr. John Ayscough's "Marotz," about which much has been said. I do not wish to labour this point. "Marotz" is not the novel of the season. I trust that I make myself plain. I shall not pronounce upon Mr. Masefield's "Captain Margaret," because, though it has been splashed all over by trowelsful of slabby and mortarish praise, it has real merits. Indeed, it has a chance of being the novel of the season. Mr. Masefield is not yet grown up. He is always trying to write "literature," and that is a great mistake. He should study the wisdom of Paul Verlaine:

"Prends l'éloquence et tords-lui son cou."

Take literature and wring its neck. I suppose that Mr. H. de Vere Stacpoole's "The Blue Lagoon" is not likely to be selected as the novel of the season. And yet, possibly, it will be the novel of the season after all, though unchosen. I will not labour this point, either. Anyone read "The Blue Lagoon" yet? Some folks have read it, for it is in its sixth edition. But when I say anyone, I mean someone, not mere folks. It might be worth looking into, "The Blue Lagoon." *Verbum sap.,* often, to Messrs. Robertson Nicoll and Shorter. In choosing "Confessio Medici" as the book of the season in general literature, Dr. Nicoll* has already come a fearful cropper, and he must regret it. I would give much to prevent him from afflicting the intelligent when the solemn annual moment arrives for him to make the reputation of a novelist. *11 July '08*

* Now Sir William Robertson Nicoll.

GERMAN EXPANSION

18 July '08 I THINK I could read anything about German Colonial expansion. The subject may not appear to be attractive; but it is. The reason lies in the fact that one is always maliciously interested in the failures of pompous and conceited persons. In the same way, one is conscious of disappointment that the Navy pother has not blossomed into a naked scandal. A naked scandal would be a bad thing, and yet one feels cheated because it has not occurred. At least I do. And I am rather human. I can glut myself on German colonial expansion—a wondrous flower. I have just read with genuine avidity M. Tonnelat's "L'Expansion Allemande hors d'Europe" (Armand Colin, 3frs. 50). It is a very good book. Most of it does not deal with colonial expansion, but with the growth and organization of Germania in the United States and Brazil. There is some delicious psychology in this part of the book. Hear the German Governor of Pennsylvania: "As for me, I consider that if the influence of the German colonist had been eliminated from Pennsylvania, Philadelphia would never have been anything but an ordinary American town like Boston, New York, Baltimore, or Chicago." M. Tonnelat gives a masterly and succinct account of the relations between Germans and native races in Africa (particularly the Herreros). It is farcical, disastrous, piquant, and grotesque. The documentation is admirably done. What can you do but smile when you gather from a table that for the murder of seven Germans by natives fifteen capital punishments and one life-imprisonment were awarded; whereas, for the murder of five natives (including a woman) by Germans, the total punishment was six and a quarter years of prison. In 1906 the amazing German Colonial Empire cost 180 millions of marks. A high price to pay for a comic opera, even with real waterfalls! M. Tonnelat has combined sobriety and exactitude with an exciting readableness. *18 July '08*

THE BOOK-BUYER

22 Aug. '08 IN the month of August, when the book trade is supposed to be dead, but which, nevertheless, sees the publication of novels by Joseph Conrad and Marie Corelli (if Joseph Conrad is one Pole, Marie Corelli is surely the other), I have had leisure to think upon the most curious of all the problems that affect the author: Who buys books? Who really does buy books? We grumble at the lack of enterprise shown by booksellers. We inveigh against that vague and long-suffering body of tradesmen because in the immortal Strand, where there are forty tobacconists, thirty-nine restaurants, half a dozen theatres, seventeen necktie shops, one Short's, and one thousand three hundred and fourteen tea cafés, there should be only two establishments for the sale of new books. We are shocked that in the whole of Regent Street it is impossible to buy a new book. We shudder when, in crossing the virgin country of the suburbs, we travel for days and never see a single bookshop. But whose fault is it that bookshops are so few? Are booksellers people who have a conscientious objection to selling books? Or is it that nobody wants to buy books?

THE BOOK-BUYER

Personally, I extract some sort of a living —a dog's existence—from the sale of books with my name on the title-page. And I am acquainted with a few other individuals who perform the same feat. I am also acquainted with a large number of individuals who have no connexion with the manufacture or distribution of literature. And when I reflect upon the habits of this latter crowd, I am astonished that I or anybody else can succeed in paying rent out of what comes to the author from the sale of books. I know scarcely a soul, I have scarcely ever met a soul, who can be said to make a habit of buying new books. I know a few souls who borrow books from Mudie's and elsewhere, and I recognize that their subscriptions yield me a trifle. But what a trifle! Do you know anybody who really buys new books? Have you ever heard tell of such a being? Of course, there are Franklinish and self-improving young men (and conceivably women) who buy cheap editions of works which the world will not willingly let die: the Temple Classics, Everyman's Library, the World's Classics, the Universal Library. Such volumes are to be found in many refined and strenuous homes—oftener unopened than opened— *22 Aug. '08*

22 Aug. '08 but still there! But does this estimable practice aid the living author to send his children to school in decent clothes? He whom I am anxious to meet is the man who will not willingly let die the author who is not yet dead. No society for the prevention of the death of corpses will help me to pay my butcher's bill.

I know that people buy motor-cars, for the newspapers are full of the dust of them. I know that they buy seats in railway-carriages and theatres, and meals at restaurants, and cravats of the new colour, and shares in companies, for they talk about their purchases, and rise into ecstasies of praise or blame concerning them. I want to learn about the people who buy new books— modest band who never praise nor blame, nor get excited over their acquisitions, preferring to keep silence, preferring to do good in secret! Let an enterprising inventor put a new tyre on the market, and every single purchaser will write to the Press and state that he has bought it and exactly what he thinks about it. Yet, though the purchasers of a fairly popular new book must be as numerous as the purchasers of a new tyre, not one of them ever " lets on " that he has purchased. I want some book-buyers to come forward and at any rate state that they have bought a book, with some account of the adventure. I should then feel partly reassured. I should know by demonstration, that a book-buyer did exist; whereas at present all I can do is to assume the existence of a book-buyer whom I have never seen, and whom nobody has ever seen. It seems to me that if a few book-buyers would kindly come forward and confess—with proper statistics—the result would be a few columns quite pleasant to read in the quietude of September. *22 Aug. '08*

JOSEPH CONRAD AND THE *ATHENÆUM*

19 Sep. '08 THE *Athenæum* is a serious journal, genuinely devoted to learning. The mischief is that it will persist in talking about literature. I do not wish to be accused of breaking a butterfly on a wheel, but the *Athenæum's* review of Mr. Joseph Conrad's new book, "A Set of Six," in its four thousand two hundred and eighteenth issue, really calls for protest. At that age the *Athenæum* ought, at any rate, to know better than to make itself ridiculous. It owes an apology to Mr. Conrad. Here we have a Pole who has taken the trouble to come from the ends of the earth to England, to learn to speak the English language, and to write it like a genius; and he is received in this grotesque fashion by the leading literary journal! Truly, the *Athenæum's* review resembles nothing so much as the antics of a provincial mayor round a foreign monarch sojourning in his town.

For, of course, the *Athenæum* is obsequious. In common with every paper in this country, it has learnt that the proper thing is to praise Mr. Conrad's work. Not to appreciate Mr. Conrad's work at this time of day would amount to bad form. There is a cliché in nearly every line of the *Athenæum's* discriminating notice. "Mr. Conrad is not the kind of author whose work one is content to meet only in fugitive form," etc. "Those who appreciate fine craftsmanship in fiction," etc. But there is worse than clichés. For example: "It is too studiously chiselled and hammered-out for that." (God alone knows for what.) Imagine the effect of studiously chiselling a work and then hammering it out! Useful process! I wonder the *Athenæum* did not suggest that Mr. Conrad, having written a story, took it to Brooklands to get it run over by a motor-car. Again: "His effects are studiously wrought, *although*—such is his mastery of literary art—they produce a swift and penetrating impression." Impossible not to recall the weighty judgment of one of Stevenson's characters upon the *Athenæum:* "Golly, what a paper!" *19 Sep. '08*

The *Athenæum* further says: "His is not at all the impressionistic method." Probably the impressionistic method is merely any method that the *Athenæum* doesn't like. But one would ask: Has it ever read the

19 Sep. '08 opening paragraph of "The Return," perhaps the most dazzling feat of impressionism in modern English? The *Athenæum* says also: "Upon the whole, we do not think the short story represents Mr. Conrad's true *métier.*" It may be that Mr. Conrad's true *métier* was, after all, that of an auctioneer; but, after "Youth," "To-morrow," "Typhoon," "Karain," "The End of the Tether," and half a dozen other mere masterpieces, he may congratulate himself on having made a fairly successful hobby of the short story. The most extraordinary of all the *Athenæum's* remarks is this: "The one ship story here, 'The Brute,' makes us regret that the author does not give us more of the sea in his work." Well, considering that about two-thirds of Mr. Conrad's work deals with the sea, considering that he has written "Lord Jim," "The Nigger of the Narcissus," "Typhoon," "Nostromo," and "The Mirror of the Sea," this regret shall be awarded the gold medal of the silly season. If the *Athenæum* were a silly paper, like the *Academy,* I should have kept an august silence on this ineptitude. But the *Athenæum* has my respect. It ought to remember the responsibilities of its position, and ought not to entrust an important work of letters to some one whose most obvious characteristic is an exquisite and profound incompetence for criticism. The explanation that occurs to me is that "A Set of Six" and "Diana Mallory" got mixed on the *Athenæum's* library table, and that each was despatched to the critic chosen for the other. *19 Sep. '08*

"A Set of Six" will not count among Mr. Conrad's major works. But in the mere use of English it shows an advance upon all his previous books. In some of his finest chapters there is scarcely a page without a phrase that no Englishman would have written, and in nearly every one of his books slight positive errors in the use of English are fairly common. In "A Set of Six" I have detected no error and extremely few questionable terms. The influence of his deep acquaintance with French is shown in the position of the adverb in "I saw again somebody in the porch." It cannot be called bad English, but it is queer. "Inasmuch that" could certainly be defended (compare "in so much that"), but an Englishman would not, I think, have written it. Nor would an Englishman be likely to write "that sort of adventures."

19 Sep. '08 Mr. Conrad still maintains his preference for indirect narrative through the mouths of persons who witnessed the events to be described. I daresay that he would justify the device with great skill and convincingness. But it undoubtedly gives an effect of clumsiness. The first story in the volume, "Gaspar Ruiz," is a striking instance of complicated narrative machinery. This peculiarity also detracts from the realistic authority of the work. For by the time you have got to the end of "A Set of Six" you have met a whole series of men who all talk just as well as Mr. Conrad writes, and upon calm reflection the existence of a whole series of such men must seem to you very improbable. The best pages in the book are those devoted to the ironical contemplation of a young lady anarchist. They are tremendous.

THE PROFESSORS

THE death of Professor Churton Collins appears to have been attended by painful circumstances, and one may be permitted to regret the disappearance from the literary arena of this vigorous pundit. He had an agreeable face, with pendant hair and the chin of a fighter. His industry must have been terrific, and personally I can forgive anything to him who consistently and violently works. He had also acquired much learning. Indeed, I should suppose that on the subject of literature he was the most learned man in Britain. Unfortunately, he was quite bereft of original taste. The root of the matter was not in him. The frowning structure of his vast knowledge overawed many people, but it never overawed an artist—unless the artist was excessively young and naïve. A man may heap up facts and facts on a given topic, and assort and label them, and have the trick of producing any particular fact at an instant's notice, and yet, despite all his efforts and honest toil, rest hopelessly among the profane. Churton Collins was such a man. He had no artistic feeling. Apart from the display of learning, which is always pleasant *26 Sep. '08*

26 Sep. '08 to the man of letters, his essays were arid and tedious. I never heard him lecture, but I should imagine that he was an ideal University Extension lecturer. I do not mean this to be in the least complimentary to him as a critic. His book, "Illustrations of Tennyson," was an entirely sterile exercise, proving on every page that the author had no real perceptions about literature. It simply made creative artists laugh. They knew. His more recent book on modern tendencies, displayed in an acute degree the characteristic inability of the typical professor to toddle alone when released from the leading-strings of tradition.

I fear that most of our professors are in a similar fix. There is Professor George Saintsbury, a regular Albert Memorial of learning. In my pensive moments I have sometimes yearned to know as many facts about literature as Professor Saintsbury knows, though he did once, I am told, state that "Wuthering Heights" was written by Charlotte. (That must have been a sadly shocking day for Mr. Clement Shorter!) I have found his Liebig "History of French Literature" very useful; it has never failed to inform me what I ought to think about the giants of the past. More important, Professor Saintsbury's critical introductions to the whole series of Dent's English edition of Balzac are startlingly just. Over and over again he hits the nail on the head and spares his finger. I have never understood by what magic he came to accomplish these prefaces. For the root of the matter is no more in Professor Saintsbury than it was in Churton Collins. He has not comprehended what he was talking about. The proof,—his style and his occasional pronouncements on questions as to which he has been quite free to make up his mind all by himself! *26 Sep. '08*

I remember one evening discussing the talents of a certain orchestral conductor, who also played the violin. I was talking to a member of his orchestra, a very genuine artist. We agreed that he had conducted badly; but, I said in his defence, "Anyhow his intentions are good. You must admit that he has a feeling for music." "My dear fellow," exclaimed the bandsman, pettishly, "no one who had any feeling for music could possibly stand the d——d row that that chap makes on the fiddle." I was silenced. I recall this episode in connexion

26 Sep. '08 with Professor Saintsbury. No one who had any feeling for literature could possibly put down the —— style that Professor Saintsbury commits. His pen could not be brought to write it. Professor Saintsbury may be as loudly positive as he likes,—his style is always quietly whispering: "Don't listen." As to his modern judgments—well for their own sakes, professors of literature ought to bind themselves by oaths never to say anything about any author who was not safely dead twenty years before they were born. Such an ordinance would at any rate ensure their dignity.

Yet another example is Professor Walter Raleigh. Fifty per cent. of you will leap up and say that I am being perverse. But I am not. It has been demonstrated to me satisfactorily, by contact with Liverpool people, that Professor Raleigh's personal influence at that university in certain ways made for righteousness. Nevertheless, Professor Raleigh has himself demonstrated to me that, wherever the root of the matter may be, it is not in *him*. One must remember that he is young, and that his underived opinions are therefore less likely to clash with the authoritative opinions of living creative artists on their contemporaries and predecessors than if he were of the same generation as the Collinses and the Saintsburys. But wait a few years. Wait until something genuinely new and original comes along and you will see what you will see. If he wished not to ruin his reputation among artists, among people who really create things, he ought not to have published his books on "Style" and on "Shakespeare." He ought to have burnt them. For they are as hollow as a drum and as unoriginal as a bride-cake: nothing but vacuity with an icing of phrases. I am brought back again to the anecdote of the musician. No one who had the least glimmering of an individual vision of what style truly is could possibly have tolerated the too fearfully ingenious mess of words that Professor Raleigh courageously calls a book on "Style." The whole thing is a flagrant contradiction of every notion of style. It may not be generally known (and I do not state it as a truth) that Professor Raleigh is a distant connection of the celebrated family of Pains, pyrotechnicians. I would begin to go to the Empire again if I could see on the programme: "10.20. Professor Raleigh, in his unique prestidigitatory performance

26 Sep. '08

26 Sep. '08 with words." Yes, I would stroll once more into the hallowed Promenade to see that. It would be amusing. But it would have no connexion with literature.

MRS. HUMPHRY WARD'S HEROINES

IT was the commercial genius of Mr. Hall Caine that invented the idea of publishing important novels during the "off" season. Miss Marie Corelli, by a sure instinct, followed suit. And now all sorts of stars, from genuine artists to mere successful artisans, take care to publish in the off season. Thus within the last few weeks we have had novels from Eden Phillpotts, Miss Beatrice Harraden, Anthony Hope, Mrs. Humphry Ward, and Miss Marie Corelli. At this rate the autumn will soon become the slack time; August will burn and throb with a six-shilling activity; publishers' clerks will form a union; and the Rt. Hon. W. F. D. Smith, M.P., who has always opposed an eight hours day, will bring in a Bill for an eight months year. *3 Oct. '08*

That a considerable social importance still attaches to the publication of a novel by Mrs. Humphry Ward may be judged from the fact that the *Manchester Guardian* specially reviewed the book on its leader page. This strange phenomenon deserves to be studied, because the *Manchester*

3 Oct. '08 *Guardian*'s reviewing easily surpasses that of any other daily paper, except, possibly, the *Times* in its Literary Supplement. The *Guardian* relies on mere, sheer intellectual power, and as a rule it does not respect persons. Its theatrical critics, for example, take joy in speaking the exact truth—never whispered in London—concerning the mandarins of the stage. Now it is remarkable that the only strictly first-class morning daily in these isles should have printed the *Guardian*'s review of "Diana Mallory" (signed "B. S."); for the article respected persons. I do not object to Mrs. Humphry Ward being reviewed with splendid prominence. I am quite willing to concede that a new book from her constitutes the matter of a piece of news, since it undoubtedly interests a large number of respectable and correct persons. A novel by Miss Marie Corelli, however, constitutes the matter of a greater piece of news; yet I have seen no review of "Holy Orders," even in a corner, in the *Guardian*. Surely the *Guardian* was not prevented from dealing faithfully with "Holy Orders" by the fact that it received no review copy, or by the fact that Miss Corelli desired no review. Its news department in general is conducted without reference to the desires of Miss Marie Corelli, and it does not usually boggle at an expenditure of four-and-sixpence. Why, then, Mrs. Humphry Ward being reviewed specially, is not Miss Marie Corelli reviewed specially? If the answer be that Mrs. Humphry Ward's novels are better, as literature, than Miss Corelli's, I submit that the answer is insufficient, and lacking in Manchester sincerity. *3 Oct. '08*

Let me duly respect Mrs. Humphry Ward. She knows her business. She is an expert in narrative. She can dress up even the silliest incidents of sentimental fiction—such as that in which the virgin heroine, in company with a young man, misses the last train home (see "Helbeck of Bannisdale")—in a costume of plausibility. She is a conscientious worker. She does not make a spectacle of herself in illustrated interviews. Even in agitating against votes for women she can maintain her dignity. (She would be an ideal President of the Authors' Society.) But, then, similar remarks apply, say, to Mr. W. E. Norris. Mr. W. E. Norris is as accomplished an expert as Mrs. Humphry Ward. He is in possession of a much better style. He has humour. He is much

3 Oct. '08 more true to life. He has never compromised the dignity of his vocation. Nevertheless, the prospect of the *Guardian* reviewing Mr. W. E. Norris on its leader-page is remote, for the reason that though he pleases respectable and correct persons, he does not please nearly so many respectable and correct persons as does Mrs. Humphry Ward. If anybody has a right to the leader-page of our unique daily, Mrs. Humphry Ward is that body. My objection to the phenomenon is that the *Guardian* falsified its item of news. It deliberately gave the impression that a serious work of art had appeared in "Diana Mallory." It ought to have known better. It did know better. If our unique daily is to yield to the snobbishness which ranks Mrs. Humphry Ward among genuine artists, where among dailies are we to look for the shadow of a great rock?

Mrs. Humphry Ward's novels are praiseworthy as being sincerely and skilfully done, but they are not works of art. They are possibly the best stuff now being swallowed by the uneducated public; and they deal with the governing classes; and when you have said that you have said all. Nothing truly serious can happen in them. It is all make-believe. No real danger of the truth about life! . . . I should think not, indeed! The fearful quandary in which the editor of *Harper's* found himself with "Jude the Obscure" was a lesson to all Anglo-Saxon editors for ever more! Mrs. Humphry Ward has never got nearer to life than, for instance, "Rita" has got—nor so near! Gladstone, a thoroughly bad judge of literature, made her reputation, and not on a postcard, either! Gladstone had no sense of humour—at any rate when he ventured into literature. Nor has Mrs. Humphry Ward. If she had she would not concoct those excruciating heroines of hers. She probably does not know that her heroines are capable of rousing temperaments such as my own to ecstasies of homicidal fury. Moreover, in literature all girls named Diana are insupportable. Look at Diana Vernon, beloved of Mr. Andrew Lang, I believe! What a creature! Imagine living with her! You can't! Look at Diana of the Crossways. Why did Diana of the Crossways marry? Nobody can say—unless the answer is that she was a ridiculous ninny. Would Anne Elliot have made such an inexplicable fool of herself? Why does Diana Mallory "go to" her preposterous Radical ex-M.P.? Simply because she is *3 Oct. '08*

3 Oct. '08 tiresomely absurd. Oh, those men with strong chins and irreproachable wristbands! Oh, those cultured conversations! Oh, those pure English maids! That skittishness! That impulsiveness! That noxious winsomeness!

I have invented a destiny for Mrs. Humphry Ward's heroines. It is terrible, and just. They ought to be caught, with their lawful male protectors, in the siege of a great city by a foreign army. Their lawful male protectors ought, before sallying forth on a forlorn hope, to provide them with a revolver as a last refuge from a brutal and licentious soldiery. And when things come to a crisis, in order to be concluded in our next, the revolvers ought to prove to be unloaded. I admit that this invention of mine is odious, and quite un-English, and such as would never occur to a right-minded subscriber to Mudie's. But it illustrates the mood caused in me by witnessing the antics of those harrowing dolls.

W. W. JACOBS AND ARISTOPHANES

I HAVE been reading a new novel by Mr. W. W. Jacobs—"Salthaven" (Methuen. 6s.). It is a long time since I read a book of his. Ministries have fallen since then, and probably Mr. Jacobs' prices have risen—indeed, much has happened—but the talent of the author of "Many Cargoes" remains steadfast where it did. "Salthaven" is a funny book. Captain Trimblett, to excuse the lateness of a friend for tea, says to the landlady: "He saw a man nearly run over!" and the landlady replies: "Yes, but how long would that take him?" If you ask me whether I consider this humorous, I reply that I do. I also consider humorous this conversational description of an exemplary boy who took to "Sandford and Merton" "as a duck takes to water": "By modelling his life on its teaching" (says young Vyner) "he won a silver medal for never missing an attendance at school. Even the measles failed to stop him. Day by day, a little more flushed than usual, perhaps, he sat in his place until the whole school was down with it, and had to be closed in consequence. Then and not till *24 Oct. '08*

24 Oct. '08 then did he feel that he had saved the situation." I care nothing for the outrageous improbability of any youthful son of a shipowner being able to talk in the brilliant fashion in which Mr. Jacobs makes Vyner talk. Success excuses it. "Salthaven" is bathed in humour.

At the same time I am dissatisfied with "Salthaven." And I do not find it easy to explain why. I suppose the real reason is that it discloses no signs of any development whatever on the part of the author. Worse, it discloses no signs of intellectual curiosity on the part of the author. Mr. Jacobs seems to live apart from the movement of his age. Nothing, except the particular type of humanity and environment in which he specializes, seems to interest him. There is no hint of a general idea in his work. By some of his fellow-artists he is immensely admired. I have heard him called, seriously, the greatest humourist, since Aristophanes. I admire him myself, and I will not swear that he is not the greatest humorist since Aristophanes. But I wil swear that no genuine humourist ever resembled Aristophanes less than Mr. Jacobs does. Aristophanes was passionately interested in everything. He would leave nothing alone. Whereas Mr. Jacobs will leave nearly everything alone. Kipling's general ideas are excessively crude, but one does feel in reading him that his curiosity is boundless, even though his taste in literature must infallibly be bad. "Q." is not to be compared in creative power with either of these two men, but one does feel in reading him that he is interested in other manifestations of his own art, that he cares for literature. Impossible to gather from Mr. Jacobs' work that he cares for anything serious at all; impossible to differentiate his intellectual outlook from that of an average reader of the *Strand Magazine!* I do not bring this as a reproach against Mr. Jacobs, whose personality it would be difficult not to esteem and to like. He cannot alter himself. I merely record the phenomenon as worthy of notice. *24 Oct. '08*

Mr. Jacobs is not alone. Among our very successful novelists, there are many like him in what I will roundly term intellectual sluggishness, though there is, perhaps, none with quite his talent. Have these men entered into a secret compact not to touch a problem even with a pair of tongs? Or

24 Oct. '08 are they afraid of being confused with Hall Caine, Mrs. Humphry Ward and Miss Marie Corelli, who anyhow have the merit of being interested in the wide aspects of their age? I do not know. But I think we might expect a little more general activity from some of our authors who lie tranquil, steeped in success as lizards in sunshine. I speak delicately, for I am on delicate ground. I do, however, speak as a creative artist, and not as a critic. Occasionally my correspondents upbraid me for not writing like a critic. I have never pretended to look at things from any other standpoint than that of a creative artist.

KENNETH GRAHAME

IT is a long time since I read a new book by Mr. Kenneth Grahame, but the fault is his rather than mine. I suppose that I was not the only reader who opened "The Wind in the Willows" (Methuen. 6s.) with an unusual and apprehensive curiosity. Would it disappoint? For really, you know, to live up to "The Golden Age" and "Pagan Papers" could not be an easy task—and after so many years of silence! It is ten years, if I mistake not, since Mr. Kenneth Grahame put his name to anything more important than the official correspondence of the Bank of England. Well, "The Wind in the Willows" does not disappoint. Here, indeed, we have the work of a man who is obviously interested in letters and in life, the work of a fastidious and yet a very robust artist. But the book is fairly certain to be misunderstood of the people. The publishers' own announcement describes it as "perhaps chiefly for youth," a description with which I disagree. The obtuse are capable of seeing in it nothing save a bread-and-butter imitation of "The Jungle Book." The woodland and sedgy lore in it is discreet and attractive. Names of animals *24 Oct. '08*

24 Oct. '08 abound in it. But it is nevertheless a book of humanity. The author may call his chief characters the Rat, the Mole, the Toad,—they are human beings, and they are meant to be nothing but human beings. Were it otherwise, the spectacle of a toad going through the motor-car craft would be merely incomprehensible and exasperating. The superficial scheme of the story is so childishly naïve, or so daringly naïve, that only a genius could have preserved it from the ridiculous. The book is an urbane exercise in irony at the expense of the English character and of mankind. It is entirely successful. Whatever may happen to it in the esteem of mandarins and professors, it will beyond doubt be considered by authentic experts as a work highly distinguished, original and amusing—and no more to be comprehended by youth than "The Golden Age" was to be comprehended by youth.

ANATOLE FRANCE

I OBTAINED the new book of Anatole France, "L'Ile des Pingouins," the day after publication, and my copy was marked "eighteenth edition." But in French publishing the word "edition" may mean anything. There is a sort of legend among the simple that it means five hundred copies. The better informed, however, are aware that it often means less. Thus, in the case of the later novels of Emile Zola, an edition meant two hundred copies. This was chiefly to save the self-love of his publishers, who did not care to admit that the idol of a capricious populace had fallen off its pedestal. The vast fiction was created that Zola sold as well as ever! One Paris firm, the "Société du Mercure de France," which in the domain of pure letters has probably issued in the last dozen years more good books than any other house in the world, has, with astounding courage, adopted the practice of numbering every copy of a book. Thus my copy of its "L'Esprit de Barbey d'Aurévilly" (an exceedingly diverting volume) is numbered 1,424. I prefer this to advertisements of "second large edition," etc. One knows where one is. But I fear the example of the *29 Oct. '08*

29 Oct. '08 Mercure de France is not likely to be honestly imitated.

If Anatole France's "editions" consist of five hundred copies I am glad. For an immediate sale of nine thousand copies is fairly remarkable when the article sold consists of nothing more solid than irony. But I am inclined to think that they do not consist of five hundred copies. There is less enthusiasm—that is to say, less genuine enthusiasm—for Anatole France than there used to be. The majority, of course, could never appreciate him, and would only buy him under the threat of being disdained by the minority, whose sole weapon is scorn. And the minority has been seriously thinking about Anatole France, and coming to the conclusion that, though a genius, he is not the only genius that ever existed. (Stendhal is at present the god of the minority of the race which the *Westminister Gazette* will persist in referring to as "our French neighbours." In some circles it is now a lapse from taste to read anything but Stendhal.) Anatole France's last two works of imagination did not brilliantly impose themselves on the intellect of his country. "L'Histoire Comique" showed once again his complete inability to construct a novel, and it appeared to be irresponsibly extravagant in its sensuality. And "Sur La Pierre Blanche" was inferior Wells. The minority has waited a long time for something large, original, and arresting; and it has not had it. The author was under no compulsion to write his history of Joan of Arc, which bears little relation to his epoch, and which one is justified in dismissing as the elegant pastime of a savant. If in Anatole France the savant has not lately flourished to the detriment of the fighting philosopher, why should he have spent years on the "Joan of Arc" at a period when Jaurès urgently needed intellectual aid against the doctrinairism of the International Congress? Jaurès was beaten, and he yielded, with the result that Clemenceau, a man far too intelligent not to be a practical Socialist at heart, has become semi-reactionary for want of support. This has not much to do with literature. Neither has the history of Joan of Arc. To return to literature, it is indubitable that Anatole France is slightly acquiring the reputation of a dilettante. *29 Oct. '08*

In "L'Ile des Pingouins" he returns, in a parable, to his epoch. For this book is the

29 Oct. '08 history of France "from the earliest time to the present day," seen in the mirror of the writer's ironical temperament. It is very good. It is inimitable. It is sheer genius. One cannot reasonably find fault with its amazing finesse. But then one is so damnably *un*reasonable! One had expected—one does not know what one had expected—but anyhow something with a more soaring flight, something more passionate, something a little less gently "tired" in its attitude towards the criminal frailties of mankind! When an A. B. Walkley yawns in print before the spectacle of the modern English theatre, it really doesn't matter. But when an Anatole France grows wearily indulgent before the spectacle of life, one is inclined to wake him by throwing "Leaves of Grass" or "Ecce Homo" (Nietzsche's) at his head. For my part, I am ready to hazard that what is wrong with Anatole France is just spiritual anæmia. Yet only a little while, and he was as great a force for pushing forward as H. G. Wells himself!

INTIMATIONS OF IMMORTALITY

THE judgments of men who have the right to judge are not as other judgments. According to Mr. Yeats " the finest comedian of his kind on the English-speaking stage " is not Mr. George Alexander, but Mr. William Fay! And who, outside Dublin, has ever heard of Mr. J. M. Synge, author of " The Playboy of the Western World " ? For myself, I have heard of him, and that is all. Mr. Yeats calls him " a unique man," and puts him above all other Irish creative artists in prose. And very probably Mr. Yeats is correct. For the difference between what informed people truly think about reputations, and what is printed about reputations by mandarins in popular papers, is apt to be startling. The other day I had a terrific pow-wow with one of the most accomplished writers now living; it occurred in the middle of a wood. We presently arrived at this point: He asked impatiently: " Well, who *is* there who can write tip-top poetry to-day? " I tried to dig out my genuine opinions. Really, it is not so easy to put one's finger on a high-class poet. I gave the names of Robert Bridges and *3 Dec. '08*

3 Dec. '08 W. B. Yeats. He wouldn't admit Mr. Yeats' tip-topness. "What about T. W. H. Crosland?" he inquired. At first, with the immeasurable and vulgar tedium of Mr. Crosland's popular books in my memory, I thought he was joking. But he was not. He was convinced that an early book by the slanger of suburbs contained as fine poetry as has been written in these days. I was formally bound over to peruse the volume. "And Alfred Douglas?" he said further. (Not that he had shares or interest in the *Academy!*) Of course, I had to admit that Lord Alfred Douglas, before he began to cut capers in the hinterland of Fleet Street, had been a poet. I have an early volume of his that, to speak mildly, I cherish. I should surmise that scarcely one person in a million has the least idea of the identity of the artists by which the end of the twentieth century will remember the beginning. The vital facts of to-day's literature always lie buried beneath chatter of large editions and immense popularities. I wouldn't mind so much, were it not incontestable that at the end of the century I shall be dead.

MALLARMÉ, BAZIN, SWINBURNE

THE Mrs. Humphry Ward of France, M. René Bazin, has visited these shores, and has been interviewed. In comparing him to Mrs. Humphry Ward, I am unfair to the lady in one sense and too generous in another. M. Bazin writes perhaps slightly better than Mrs. Humphry Ward, but not much. *Per contra,* he is a finished master of the art of self-advertisement, whereas the public demeanour of Mrs. Humphry Ward is entirely beyond reproach. M. Bazin did not get through his interview without giving some precise statistical information as to the vast sale of his novels. I suppose that M. Bazin, Academician and apostle of literary correctitude, is just the type of official mediocrity that the Alliançe Française was fated to invite to London as representative of French letters. My only objection to the activities of M. Bazin is that, not content with a golden popularity, he cannot refrain from sneering at genuine artists. Thus, to the interviewer, he referred to Stéphane Mallarmé as a "fumiste." No English word will render exactly this French slang; it may be roughly translated *17 Dec. '08*

17 Dec. '08 as a practical joker with a trace of fraud. There may be, and there are, two opinions as to the permanent value of Mallarmé's work, but there cannot be two informed and honest opinions as to his profound sincerity. It is indubitable that he had one aim—to produce the finest literature of which he was capable, and that to this aim he sacrificed everything else in his career. A charming spectacle, this nuncio of mediocrity and of the Académie Française coming to London to assert that a distinguished writer like Mallarmé was a "fumiste"! If anyone wishes to know what is thought of Mallarmé by the younger French school, let him read the Mallarmé chapter in André Gide's "Prétextes." In this very able book will be found also some wonderful reminiscences of Oscar Wilde.

Speaking of the respect which ought to be accorded to a distinguished artist, there is an excellent example of propriety in Dr. Levin Schücking's review of Swinburne's "The Age of Shakespeare," which brings to a close the extraordinarily fine first number of the *English Review.* Dr. Schücking shows that he is quite aware of the defects of manner which mark the book, but his own manner is the summit of courteous deference such as is due to one of the chief ornaments of English literature, and to a very old man. "A Man of Kent" (*British Weekly*), in commenting on the article, regrets its timidity, and refers to Swinburne as the "howling dervish" of criticism. This is the kind of lapse from decorum which causes the judicious not to grieve but to shrug their shoulders. Probably "A Man of Kent" would wish to withdraw it. I trust he is aware that "The Age of Shakespeare" is packed full of criticism whose insight and sensitiveness no other English critic could equal. *17 Dec. '08*

THE RUINED SEASON

24 Dec. '08 IN a recent number of the *Athenæum* appeared a letter from Mr. E. H. Cooper, novelist and writer for children, protesting against the publication of the Queen's Gift-Book and the royally-commanded cheap edition of Queen Victoria's Letters during the autumn season, and requesting their Majesties to forbear next year from injuring the general business of books as they have injured it this year. That some semi-official importance is attached to Mr. Cooper's statements is obvious from the fact that the *Athenæum* (which is the organ of the trade as well as of learning) thought well to print his letter. But Mr. Cooper undoubtedly exaggerates. He states that the two books in question "have ruined the present publishing season rather more effectively than a Pan-European war could have done." Briefly, this is ridiculous. He says further: "Men and women who could trust to a sale of 5000 or 6000 copies of a novel, equally with authors who can command much larger sales, find that this year the sale of their annual novel has reached a tenth part of the usual figures." This also is ridiculous. The general view is that, while the season has been scarcely up to the average for fiction, it has not been below the average on the whole. But Mr. Cooper is nothing if not sweeping. A few days later he wrote to the *Westminster Gazette* about the House of Lords, and said: "I am open to wager a considerable sum that if the Government fights a general election next year they will win back all their lost by-elections and get an increased majority besides." Such rashness proves that grammar is not Mr. Cooper's only weak point. *24 Dec. '08*

It is a pity that Mr. Cooper's protest was not made with more moderation, for it was a protest worth making. The books of the two Queens have not ruined the season, nor have they reduced the sales of popular novels by 90 per cent.; but they have upset trade quite unnecessarily. The issue of "Queen Victoria's Letters" at six shillings was a worthy idea, but its execution was thoughtlessly timed. The volumes would have sold almost equally well at another period of the year. As for "Queen Alexandra's Gift-Book," I personally have an objection to the sale of books for charity, just as I have an objection to all indirect taxation and to the paying of rates out of

24 Dec. '08 gas profits. In such enterprises as the vast, frenzied pushing and booming of the "Gift-Book," the people who really pay are just the people who get no credit whatever. The public who buy get rich value for their outlay; the chief pushers and boomsters get an advertisement after their own hearts; and the folk who genuinely but unwillingly contribute, without any return of any kind, are authors whose market is disturbed and booksellers who, partly intimidated and partly from good nature, handle the favoured book on wholesale terms barely profitable. I will have none of Mr. Cooper's 90 per cent.; but I daresay that I have lost at the very least £10 owing to the "Gift-Book." That is to say, I have furnished £10 to the Unemployed Fund. I share Mr. Cooper's resentment. I do not want to give £10 to any fund whatever, and to force me to pay it to the Unemployed Fund, of all funds, is to insult my most sacred convictions. £10 wants earning. And the fact that £10 wants earning should be brought to the attention of Windsor and Greeba Castles.

Still, I am not depressed about the general cause of serious literature. Serious literature is kept alive by a few authors who, not owning motor-cars nor entertaining parties to dinner at the Carlton, find it possible and agreeable to maintain life and decency on the money paid down by very small bands of truly bookish readers. And these readers are not likely to deprive themselves completely of literature for ever in order to possess a collection of royal photographs. The injury to serious literature is slight and purely temporary. *24 Dec. '08*

A melancholy Christmas, it seems! According to "a well-known member of the trade," the business is once again—the second time this year—about to crumble into ruins. This well-known member of the trade, who discreetly refrains from signing his name, writes to the *Athenæum* in answer to Mr. E. H. Cooper's letter about the disastrous influence of royal books on the publishing season. According to him, Mr. Cooper is all wrong. The end of profitable publishing is being brought about, not by their Majesties, but once more by the authors and their agents. It appears that too many books are published. Authors and their agents have evidently some miraculous method of forcing publishers to publish books which they do not want to *31 Dec. '08*

31 Dec. '08 publish. I am not a member of the trade, but I should have thought that few things could be easier than not to publish a book. Presumably the agent stands over the publisher with a contract in one hand and a revolver in the other, and, after a glance at the revolver, the publisher signs without glancing at the contract. Secondly, it appears, authors and their agents habitually compel the publisher to pay too much, so that he habitually publishes at a loss. (Novels, that is.) I should love to know how the trick is done, but a well-known member of the trade does not go into details. He merely states the broad fact. Thirdly, the sevenpenny reprint of the popular novel is ruining the already-ruined six-shilling novel. It is comforting to perceive that this wickedness on the part of the sevenpenny reprint cannot indefinitely continue. For when there are no six-shilling novels to reprint, obviously there can be no sevenpenny reprints of them. There is justice in England yet; but a well-known member of the trade has not noticed that the sevenpenny novel, in killing its own father, must kill itself. At any rate he does not refer to the point.

THE RUINED SEASON

I have been young, and now am nearly old. *31 Dec. '08* Silvered is the once-brown hair. Dim is the eye that on a time could decipher minion type by moonlight. But never have I seen the publisher without a fur coat in winter nor his seed begging bread. Nor do I expect to see such sights. Yet I have seen an author begging bread, and instead of bread, I gave him a railway-ticket. Authors have always been in the wrong, and they always will be: grasping, unscrupulous, mercernary creatures that they are! Some of them haven't even the wit to keep their books from being burnt at the stake by the executioners of the National Vigilance Association. I wonder that publishers don't dispense with them altogether, and carry on unaided the great tradition of English literature. Anyhow, publishers have had my warm sympathy this Christmas time. When I survey myself, as an example, lapped in luxury and clinking multitudinous gold coins extorted from publishers by my hypnotizing rascal of an agent; and when I think of the publishers, endeavoring in their fur coats to keep warm in fireless rooms and picking turkey limbs while filling up bankruptcy forms—I blush. Or I should blush, were not authors notoriously incapable of that action.

1909

"ECCE HOMO"

THE people who live in the eye of the public have been asked, as usual, to state what books during the past year have most interested them, and they have stated. This year I think the lists are less funny than usual. But some items give joy. Thus the Bishop of London has read Mr. A. E. W. Mason's "The Broken Road" with interest and pleasure. Mr. Frederic Harrison, along with two historical works, has read "Diana Mallory" with interest and pleasure. What an unearthly light such confessions throw upon the mentalities from which they emanate! As regards the Bishop of London I should not have been surprised to hear that he had read "Holy Orders" with interest and pleasure. But Mr. Frederic Harrison, one had naïvely imagined, possessed some rudimentary knowledge of the art which he has practised. *7 Jan. '09*

This confessing malady is infectious, if not contagious. I suppose that few persons can resist the microbe. I cannot. I feel compelled to announce to all whom it may not concern the books of the year which (at the moment of writing) seem to have most interested me—apart from my own, *bien*

7 Jan. '09 *entendu*: H. G. Wells's "New Worlds for Old." If it is not in its fiftieth thousand the intelligent masses ought to go into a month's sackcloth. "Nature Poems," by William H. Davies. This slim volume is quite indubitably wondrous. I won't say that it contains some of the most lyrical lyrics in English, but I will say that there are lyrics in it as good as have been produced by anybody at all in the present century. "A Poor Man's House," by Stephen Reynolds. Young Mr. Reynolds has already been fully accepted by the aforesaid intelligent masses, and I have no doubt that he is tolerably well satisfied with 1908. Nietzsche's "Ecce Homo." When this book gets translated into English (I have been reading it in Henri Albert's French translation) it will assuredly be laughed at. I would hazard that it is the most conceited book ever written. Take our four leading actor-managers; extract from them all their conceit; multiply that conceit by the self-satisfaction of Mr. F. E. Smith, M.P. when he has made a joke; and raise the result to the Kaiser-power, and you will have something less than the cube-root of Nietzsche's conceit in this the last book he wrote. But it is a great book, full of great things.

HENRY OSPOVAT

THE death of that distinguished draughtsman and painter, Henry Ospovat, who was among the few who can illustrate a serious author without insulting him, ought not to pass unnoticed. Because an exhibition of his caricatures made a considerable stir last year it was generally understood that he was destined exclusively for caricature. But he was a man who could do several things very well indeed, and caricature was only one of these things. In Paris he would certainly have made a name and a fortune as a caricaturist. They have more liberty there. Witness Rouveyre's admirable and appalling sketch of Sarah Bernhardt in the current "Mercure de France." I never met Ospovat, but I was intimate with some of his friends while he was at South Kensington. In those days I used to hear "what Ospovat thought" about everything. He must have been listened to with great respect by his fellow-students. And sometimes one of them would come to me, with the air of doing me a favour (as indeed he was) and say: "Look here. Do you want to buy something good, at simply no price at all?" And I became the possessor of a beautiful sketch by *14 Jan. '09*

14 Jan. '09 Ospovat, while the intermediary went off with a look on his face as if saying: "Consider yourself lucky, my boy!" I used even to get Ospovat's opinions on my books, now and then very severe. I wanted to meet him. But I never could. The youths used to murmur: "Oh! It's no use you *meeting* him." They were afraid he was not spectacular enough. Or they desired to keep him to themselves, like a precious pearl. I pictured him as very frail, and very positive in a quiet way. He was only about thirty when he died last week.

FRENCH AND BRITISH ACADEMIES

ALTHOUGH we know in our hearts that the French Academy is a foolish institution, designed and kept up for the encouragement of mediocrity, correct syntax, and the *status quo,* we still, also in our hearts, admire it and watch its mutations with the respect which we always give to foreign phenomena and usually withold from phenomena British. The last-elected member is M. Francis Charmes. His sole title to be an Academician is that he directs "La Revue des deux Mondes," which pays good prices to Academic contributors. And this is, of course, a very good title. Even his official "welcomer," M. Henry Houssaye, did not assert that M. Charmes had ever written anything more important or less mortal than leaders and paragraphs in the "Journal des Débâtes." M. Henry Houssaye was himself once a journalist. But he thought better of that, and became a historian. He has written one or two volumes which, without being unreadable, have achieved immense popularity. Stevenson used to delve in them for matter suitable to his romances. The French Academy now contains pretty *21 Jan. '09*

21 Jan. '09 nearly everything except first-class literary artists. Anatole France is a first-class literary artist and an Academician; but he makes a point of never going near the Academy. Perhaps the best writer among "devout" Academicians is Maurice Barrès. Unhappily his comic-opera politics prove that in attempting Parnassus he mistook his mountain. Primrose Hill would have been more in his line. Still, he wrote "Le Jardin de Bérénice": a novel which I am afraid to read again lest I should fail to recapture the first fine careless rapture it gave me.

Personally, I think our British Academy is a far more brilliant affair than the French. There is no nonsense about it. At least very little, except Mr. Balfour. I believe, from inductive processes of thought, that when Mr. Balfour gets into his room of a night he locks the door—and smiles. Not the urbane smile that fascinates and undoes even Radical journalists—quite another smile. Never could this private smile have been more subtle than on the night of the day when he permitted himself to be elected a member of the British Academy. Further, let it not be said that our Academy excludes novelists and journalists. We novelists are ably represented by Mr. Andrew Lang, author of "Prince Prigio" and part-author of "The World's Desire." And we journalists have surely an adequate spokesman in the person of the author of "Lost Leaders." Mr. Lang has also dabbled in history. *21 Jan. '09*

POE AND THE SHORT STORY

28 Jan. '09 THE great Edgar Allan Poe celebration has passed off, and no one has been seriously hurt by the terrific display of fireworks. Some of the set pieces were pretty fair; for example, Mr. G. B. Shaw's in the *Nation* and Prof. C. H. Herford's in the *Manchester Guardian*. On the whole, however, the enthusiasm was too much in the nature of mere good form. If only we could have a celebration of Omar Khayyam, Tennyson, Gilbert White, or the inventor of Bridge, the difference between new and manufactured enthusiasm would be apparent. We have spent several happy weeks in conceitedly explaining to that barbaric race, the Americans, that in Poe they have never appreciated their luck. Yet we ourselves have never understood Poe. And we never shall understand Poe. It is immensely to our credit that, owing to the admirable obstinacy of Mr. J. H. Ingram, we now admit that Poe was neither a drunkard, a debauchee, nor a cynical eremite. This is about as far as we shall get. Poe's philosophy of art, as discovered in his essays and his creative work, is purely Latin and, as such, incomprehensible and even naughty to the Saxon mind. To the average bookish Englishman Poe means "The Pit and the Pendulum," and his finest poetry means nothing at all. Tell that Englishman that Poe wrote more beautiful lyrics than Tennyson, and he will blankly put you down as mad. (So shall I.) *28 Jan. '09*

Once, and not many years since, I contemplated editing a complete edition of Poe, with a brilliant introduction in which I was to show that the appearance of a temperament like his in the United States in the early years of the nineteenth century was the most puzzling miracle that can be found in the whole history of literature. Then, naturally, I intended to explain the miracle. My plans were placed before a wise and good publisher, whose reply was to indicate two very respectable complete editions of Poe which had eminently failed with the public. Further enquiries satisfied me that the public had no immediate use for anything elaborate, final, and expensive concerning Poe. My bright desire therefore paled and flickered out. Since then I have come to the conclusion that I know practically nothing of the "secret of Poe," and that nobody else knows much more.

28 Jan. '09 It was inevitable that, apropos of Poe, our customary national nonsense about the "art of the short story" should have recurred in a painful and acute form. It is a platitude of "Literary Pages" that Anglo-Saxon writers cannot possess themselves of the "art of the short story." The only reason advanced has been that Guy de Maupassant wrote very good short stories, and he was French! God be thanked! Last week we all admitted that Poe had understood the "art of the short story." (His name had not occurred to us before.) Henceforward our platitude will be that no Anglo-Saxon writer can compass the "art of the short story" unless his name happens to be Poe. Another platitude is that the short story is mysteriously somehow more difficult than the long story—the novel. Whenever I meet that phrase, "art of the short story," in the press I feel as if I had drunk mustard-and-water. And I would like here to state that there are as good short stories in English as in any language, and that the whole theory of the unsuitability of English soil to that trifling plant the short story is ridiculous. Nearly every novelist of the nineteenth century, from Scott to Stevenson, wrote first-class short stories. There are now working in England to-day at least six writers who can write, and have written, better short stories than any living writer of their age in France. As for the greater difficulty of the short story, ask any novelist who has succeeded equally well in both. Ask Thomas Hardy, ask George Meredith ask Joseph Conrad, ask H. G. Wells, ask Murray Gilchrist, ask George Moore, ask Eden Phillpotts, ask "Q.," ask Henry James. Lo! I say to all facile gabblers about the "art of the short story," as the late "C. B." said to Mr. Balfour: "Enough of this foolery!" It is of a piece with the notion that a fine sonnet is more difficult than a fine epic. *28 Jan. '09*

MIDDLE-CLASS

4 Feb. '09 As a novelist, a creative artist working in the only literary "form" which widely appeals to the public, I sometimes wonder curiously what the public is. Not often, because it is bad for the artist to think often about the public. I have never by enquiry from those experts my publishers learnt anything useful or precise about the public. I hear the words "the public," "the public," uttered in awe or in disdain, and this is all. The only conclusion which can be drawn from what I am told is that the public is the public. Still, it appears that my chief purchasers are the circulating libraries. It appears that without the patronage of the circulating libraries I should either have to live on sixpence a day or starve. Hence, when my morbid curiosity is upon me, I stroll into Mudie's or the Times Book Club, or I hover round Smith's bookstall at Charing Cross.

The crowd at these places is the prosperous crowd, the crowd which grumbles at income-tax and pays it. Three hundred and seventy-five thousand persons paid income-tax last year, under protest: they stand for the existence of perhaps a million souls, and this million is a handful floating more or less easily on the surface of the forty millions of the population. The great majority of my readers must be somewhere in this million. There can be few hirers of books who neither pay income-tax nor live on terms of dependent equality with those who pay it. I see at the counters people on whose foreheads it is written that they know themselves to be the salt of the earth. Their assured, curt voices, their proud carriage, their clothes, the similarity of their manners, all show that they belong to a caste and that the caste has been successful in the struggle for life. It is called the middle-class, but it ought to be called the upper-class, for nearly everything is below it. I go to the Stores, to Harrod's Stores, to Barker's, to Rumpelmeyer's, to the Royal Academy, and and to a dozen clubs in Albemarle Street and Dover Street, and I see again just the same crowd, well-fed, well-dressed, completely free from the cares which beset at least five-sixths of the English race. They have worries; they take taxis because they must not indulge in motor-cars, hansoms because taxis are an extravagance, and omnibuses because they really must economise. But they never look twice at twopence. They curse the *4 Feb. '09*

4 Feb. '09 injustice of fate, but secretly they are aware of their luck. When they have nothing to do, they say, in effect: "Let's go out and spend something." And they go out. They spend their lives in spending. They deliberately gaze into shop windows in order to discover an outlet for their money. You can catch them at it any day.

I do not belong to this class by birth. Artists very seldom do. I was born slightly beneath it. But by the help of God and strict attention to business I have gained the right of entrance into it. I admit that I have imitated its deportment, with certain modifications of my own; I think its deportment is in many respects worthy of imitation. I am acquainted with members of it; some are artists like myself; a few others win my sympathy by honestly admiring my work; and the rest I like because I like them. But the philosopher in me cannot, though he has tried, melt away my profound and instinctive hostility to this class. Instead of decreasing, my hostility grows. I say to myself: "I can never be content until this class walks along the street in a different manner, until that now absurd legend has been worn clean off its forehead." Henry Harland was not a great writer, but he said: *Il faut souffrir pour être sel.* I ask myself impatiently: "When is this salt going to begin to suffer?" That is my attitude towards the class. I frequent it but little. Nevertheless I know it intimately, nearly all the intimacy being on my side. For I have watched it during long, agreeable sardonic months and years in foreign hotels. In foreign hotels you get the essence of it, if not the cream. *4 Feb. '09*

Chief among its characteristics—after its sincere religious worship of money and financial success—I should put its intense self-consciousness as a class. The world is a steamer in which it is travelling saloon. Occasionally it goes to look over from the promenade deck at the steerage. Its feelings towards the steerage are kindly. But the tone in which it says "the steerage" cuts the steerage off from it more effectually than many bulkheads. You perceive also from that tone that it could never be surprised by anything that the steerage might do. Curious social phenomenon, the steerage! In the saloon there runs a code, the only possible code, the final code; and it is

4 Feb. '09 observed. If it is not observed, the infraction causes pain, distress. Another marked characteristic is its gigantic temperamental dullness, unresponsiveness to external suggestion, a lack of humour—in short, a heavy and half-honest stupidity; ultimate product of gross prosperity, too much exercise, too much sleep. Then I notice a grim passion for the *status quo.* This is natural. Let these people exclaim as they will against the structure of society, the last thing they desire is to alter it. This passion shows itself in naïve admiration for everything that has survived its original usefulness, such as sail-drill and uniforms. Its mirror of true manhood remains that excellent and appalling figure, the Brushwood Boy. The passion for the *status quo* also shows itself in a general defensive, sullen hatred of all ideas whatever. You cannot argue with these people. "Do you really think so?" they will politely murmur, when you have asserted your belief that the earth is round, or something like that. And their tone says: "Would you mind very much if we leave this painful subject? My feelings on it are too deep for utterance." Lastly, I am impressed by their attitude towards the artist, which is mediæval, or perhaps Roman. Blind to nearly every form of beauty, they scorn art, and scorning art they scorn artists. It was this class which, at inaugurations of public edifices, invented the terrible toast-formula, "The architect *and contractor.*" And if epics were inaugurated by banquet, this class would certainly propose the health of the poet and printer, after the King and the publishers. Only sheer ennui sometimes drives it to seek distraction in the artist's work. It prefers the novelist among artists because the novel gives the longest surcease from ennui at the least expenditure of money and effort. *4 Feb. '09*

It is inevitable that I shall be accused of exaggeration, cynicism, or prejudice: probably all three. Whenever one tells the truth in this island of compromise, one is sure to be charged on these counts, and to be found guilty. But I too am of the sporting race, and forty years have taught me that telling the truth is the most dangerous and most glorious of all forms of sport. Alpine climbing in winter is nothing to it. I like it. I will only add that I have been speaking of the solid *bloc* of the caste; I admit the existence of a broad fringe of exceptions. And I truly sympathize with the *bloc*. I do

4 Feb. '09 not blame the *bloc*. I know that the members of the *bloc* are, like me, the result of evolutionary forces now spent. My hostility to the *bloc* is beyond my control, an evolutionary force gathering way. Upon my soul, I love the *bloc*. But when I sit among it, clothed in correctness, and reflect that the *bloc* maintains me and mine in a sort of comfort, because I divert its leisure, the humour of the situation seems to me enormous.

11 Feb. '09 I continue my notes on the great stolid comfortable class which forms the backbone of the novel-reading public. The best novelists do not find their material in this class. Thomas Hardy, never. H. G. Wells, almost never; now and then he glances at it ironically, in an episodic manner. Hale White (Mark Rutherford), never. Rudyard Kipling, rarely; when he touches it, the reason is usually because it happens to embrace the military caste, and the result is usually such mawkish stories as "William the Conqueror" and "The Brushwood Boy." J. M. Barrie, never. W. W. Jacobs, never. Murray Gilchrist, never. Joseph Conrad, never. Leonard Merrick, very slightly. George Moore, in a "Drama in

Muslin," wrote a masterpiece about it twenty years ago; "Vain Fortune" is also good; but for a long time it had ceased to interest the artist in him, and his very finest work ignores it. George Meredith was writing greatly about it thirty years ago. Henry James, with the chill detachment of an outlander, fingers the artistic and cosmopolitan fringe of it. In a rank lower than these, we have William de Morgan and John Galsworthy. The former does not seem to be inspired by it. As for John Galsworthy, the quality in him which may possibly vitiate his right to be considered a major artist is precisely his fierce animosity to this class. Major artists are seldom so cruelly hostile to anything whatever as John Galsworthy is to this class. He does in fiction what John Sargent does in paint; and their inimical observation of their subjects will gravely prejudice both of them in the eyes of posterity. I think I have mentioned all the novelists who have impressed themselves at once on the public and genuinely on the handful of persons whose taste is severe and sure. There may be, there are, other novelists alive whose work will end by satisfying the tests of the handful. Whether any of these others deal mainly with the *4 Feb. '09*

4 Feb. '09 superior stolid comfortable, I cannot certainly say; but I think not. I am ready to assert that in quite modern English fiction there exists no large and impartial picture of the superior stolid comfortable which could give pleasure to a reader of taste. Rather hard on the class that alone has made novel-writing a profession in which a man can earn a reasonable livelihood!

The explanation of this state of affairs is obscure. True, that distinguished artists are very seldom born into the class. But such an explanation would be extremely inadequate. Artists often move creatively with ease far beyond the boundaries of their native class. Thomas Hardy is not a peasant, nor was Stendhal a marquis. I could not, with any sort of confidence, offer an explanation. I am, however, convinced that only a supreme artist could now handle successfully the material presented by the class in question. The material itself lacks interest, lacks essential vitality, lacks both moral and spectacular beauty. It powerfully repels the searcher after beauty and energy. It may be in a decay. One cannot easily recall a great work of art of which the subject is decadence.

MIDDLE-CLASS

The backbone of the novel-reading public is excessively difficult to please, and rarely capable of enthusiasm. Listen to Mudie subscribers on the topic of fiction and you will scarcely ever hear the accent of unmixed pleasure. It is surprising how even favourites are maltreated in conversation. Some of the most successful favourites seem to be hated, and to be read under protest. The general form of approval is a doubtful "Ye-es!" with a whole tail of unspoken "buts" lying behind it. Occasionally you catch the ecstatic note, "Oh! *Yes;* a *sweet* book!" Or, with masculine curtness: "Fine book, that!" (For example, "The Hill," by Horace Annesley Vachell!) It is in the light of such infrequent exclamations that you may judge the tepid reluctance of other praise. The reason of all this is twofold; partly in the book, and partly in the reader. The backbone dislikes the raising of any question which it deems to have been decided: a peculiarity which at once puts it in opposition to all fine work, and to nearly all passable second-rate work. It also dislikes being confronted with anything that it considers "unpleasant," that is to say, interesting. It has a genuine horror of the truth neat. It quite honestly *11 Feb. '09*

11 Feb. '09 asks "to be taken out of itself," unaware that to be taken out of itself is the very last thing it really desires. What it wants is to be confirmed in itself. Its religion is the *status quo*. The difficulties of the enterprise of not offending it either in subject or treatment are, perhaps, already sufficiently apparent. But incomparably the greatest obstacle to pleasing it lies in the positive fact that it prefers not to be pleased. It undoubtedly objects to the very sensations which an artist aims to give. If I have heard once, I have heard fifty times resentful remarks similar to: "I'm not going to read any more bosh by *him!* Why, I simply couldn't put the thing down!" It is profoundly hostile to art, and the empire of art. It will not willingly yield. Its attitude to the magic spell is its attitude to the dentist's gas-bag. This is the most singular trait that I have discovered in the backbone.

Why, then, does the backbone put itself to the trouble of reading current fiction? The answer is that it does so, not with any artistic, spiritual, moral, or informative purpose, but simply in order to pass time. Lately, one hears, it has been neglecting fiction in favour of books of memoirs, often scandalous, and historical compilations, for the most part scandalous sexually. That it should tire of the fiction offered to it is not surprising, seeing that it so seldom gets the fiction of its dreams. The supply of good, workmanlike fiction is much larger to-day than ever it was in the past. The same is to be said of the supply of genuinely distinguished fiction. But the supply of fiction which really appeals to the backbone of the fiction-reading public is far below the demand. The backbone grumbles, but it continues to hire the offensive stuff, because it cannot obtain sufficient of the inoffensive,—and time hangs so heavy! The caprice for grape-nut history and memoirs cannot endure, for it is partially a pose. Besides, the material will run short. After all, Napoleon only had a hundred and three mistresses, and we are already at Mademoiselle Georges. The backbone, always loyal to its old beliefs, will return to fiction with a new gusto, and the cycle of events will recommence. *11 Feb. '09*

But it is well for novelists to remember that, in the present phase of society and mechanical conditions of the literary market their professional existence depends on the fact that the dullest class in England takes to

11 Feb. '09 novels merely as a refuge from its own dullness. And while it is certain that no novelist of real value really pleases that class, it is equally certain that without its support (willing or unwilling—usually the latter), no novelist could live by his pen. Remove the superior stolid comfortable, and the circulating libraries would expire. And exactly when the circulating libraries breathed their last sigh the publishers of fiction would sympathetically give up the ghost. If you happen to be a literary artist, it makes you think—the reflection that when you dine you eat the bread unwillingly furnished by the enemies of art and of progress.

THE POTENTIAL PUBLIC

I WANT to dig a little deeper through the strata of the public. Below the actual fiction-reading public which I have described, there is a much vaster potential public. It exists in London, and it exists also in the provinces. I will describe it as I have found it in the industrial midlands and north. Should the picture seem black, let me say that my picture of a similar public in London would be even blacker. In all essential qualities I consider the lower middle-class which regards, say, Manchester as its centre, to be superior to the lower middle-class which regards Charing Cross as its centre. *18 Feb, '09*

All around Manchester there are groups of municipalities which lie so close to one another that each group makes one town. Take a medium group comprising a quarter of a million inhabitants, with units ranging from sixty down to sixteen thousand. I am not going to darken my picture with a background of the manual workers, the immense majority of whom never read anything that costs more than a penny—unless it be "Gale's Special." I will deal only with the comparatively enlightened crust—employers,

18 Feb. '09 clerks, officials, and professional men, and their families—which has formed on the top of the mass, with an average income of possibly two hundred per annum per family. This crust is the élite of the group. It represents its highest culture, and in bulk it is the "lower middle-class" of Tory journalism. In London some of the glitter of the class above it is rubbed on to it by contact. One is apt to think that because there are bookshops in the Strand and large circulating libraries in Oxford Street, and these thoroughfares are thronged with the lower middle-class, therefore the lower middle-class buys or hires books. In my industrial group the institutions and machinery perfected by the upper class for itself do not exist at all, and one may watch the lower without danger of being led to false conclusions by the accidental propinquity of phenomena that have really nothing whatever to do with it.

Now in my group of a quarter of a million souls there is not a single shop devoted wholly or principally to the sale of books. Not one. You might discover a shop specializing in elephants or radium; but a real bookshop does not exist. In a town of forty thousand inhabitants there will be a couple of stationers, whose chief pride is that they are "steam printers" or lithographers. Enter their shops, and you will see a few books. Tennyson in gilt. Volumes of the Temple Classics or Everyman. Hymn books, Bibles. The latest cheap Shakespeare. Of new books no example except the brothers Hocking. The stationer will tell you that there is no demand for books; but that he can procure anything you specially want by return of post. He will also tell you that on the whole he makes no profit out of books; what trifle he captures on his meagre sales he loses on books unsold. He may inform you that his rival has entirely ceased to stock books of any sort, and that he alone stands for letters in the midst of forty thousand people. In a town of sixty thousand there will be a largeish stationer's with a small separate book department. Contents similar to the other shop, with a fair selection of cheap reprints, and half a dozen of the most notorious new novels, such as novels by Marie Corelli, Max Pemberton, Mrs. Humphry Ward. That is all. Both the shops described will have two or three regular book-buying clients, not more than ten in *18 Feb. '09*

18 Feb. '09 a total of a hundred thousand. These ten are book-lovers. They follow the book lists. They buy to the limit of their purses. And in the cult of literature they keep themselves quite apart from the society of the town, despising it. The town is simply aware that they are "great readers."

Another agency for the radiation of light in the average town first mentioned is the Municipal Free Library. The yearly sum spent on it is entirely inadequate to keep it up-to-date. A fraction of its activity is beneficial, as much to the artisan as to members of the crust. But the chief result of the penny-in-the-pound rate is to supply women old and young with outmoded, viciously respectable, viciously sentimental fiction. A few new novels get into the Library every year. They must, however, be "innocuous," that is to say, devoid of original ideas. This, of course, is inevitable in an institution presided over by a committee which has infinitely less personal interest in books than in politics or the price of coal. No Municipal Library can hope to be nearer than twenty-five years to date. Go into the average good home of the crust, in the quietude of "after-tea," and you will see a youthful miss sitting over something *18 Feb. '09* by Charlotte M. Yonge or Charles Kingsley. And that something is repulsively foul, greasy, sticky, black. Remember that it reaches from thirty to a hundred such good homes every year. Can you wonder that it should carry deposits of jam, egg, butter, coffee, and personal dirt? You cannot. But you are entitled to wonder why the Municipal Sanitary Inspector does not inspect it and order it to be destroyed. . . . That youthful miss in torpidity over that palimpsest of filth is what the Free Library has to show as the justification of its existence. I know what I am talking about.

A third agency is the book-pedlar. There are firms of publishers who never advertise in any literary weekly or any daily, who never publish anything new, and who may possibly be unknown to Simpkins themselves. They issue badly-printed, badly bound, showy editions of the eternal Scott and the eternal Dickens, in many glittering volumes with scores of bleared illustrations, and they will sell them up and down the provinces by means of respectably dressed "commission agents," at prices much in excess of their value, to an ingenuous,

18 Feb. '09 ignorant public that has never heard of Dent and Routledge. The books are found in houses where the sole function of literature is to flatter the eye. The ability of these subterranean firms to dispose of deplorable editions to persons who do not want them is in itself a sharp criticism of the commercial organization of the more respectable trade.

Let it not be supposed that my group is utterly cut off from the newest developments in imaginative prose literature. No! What the bookseller, the book-pedlar, and the Free Library have failed to do, has been accomplished by Mr. Jesse Boot, incidentally benefactor of the British provinces and the brain of a large firm of chemists and druggists with branches in scores, hundreds, of towns. He has several branches in my group. Each branch has a circulating library, patronized by the class which has only heard of Mudie, and has not heard of the Grosvenor. Mr. Jesse Boot has had the singular and beautiful idea of advertising his wares by lending books to customers and non-customers at a loss of ten thousand a year. His system is simplicity and it is cheapness. He is generous. If you desire a book which he has not got in stock he will buy it and lend it to you for twopence. *18 Feb. '09* Thus in the towns of my group the effulgent centre of culture is the chemist's shop. The sole point of contact with living literature is the chemist's shop. A wonderful world, this England! Two things have principally struck me about Mr. Jesse Boot's * clients. One is that they are usually women, and the other is that they hire their books at haphazard, nearly in the dark, with no previous knowledge of what is good and what is bad.

It is to be added that the tremendous supply of sevenpenny bound volumes of modern fiction, and of shilling bound volumes of modern belles-lettres (issued by Nelsons and others) is producing a demand in my group, is, in fact, making book-buyers where previously there were no book-buyers. These tomes now rival the works of the brothers Hocking in the stationer's shop. Their standard is decidedly above the average, owing largely to the fact that the guide-in-chief of Messrs. Nelsons happens to be a genuine man of letters. I am told that Messrs. Nelsons alone sell twenty thousand volumes a week. Yet even they have but

* Now Sir Jesse Boot.

18 Feb. '09 scratched the crust. The crust is still only the raw material of a new book public.

If it is cultivated and manufactured with skill it will surpass immeasurably in quantity, and quite appreciably in quality, the actual book-public. One may say that the inception of the process has been passably good. One is inclined to prophesy that within a moderately short period—say a dozen years—the centre of gravity of the book market will be rudely shifted. But the event is not yet.

H. G. WELLS

WELLS! I have heard that significant monosyllable pronounced in various European countries, and with various bizarre accents. And always there was admiration, passionate or astonished, in the tone. But the occasion of its utterance which remains historic in my mind was in England. I was, indeed, in Frank Richardson's Bayswater. "Wells?" exclaimed a smart, positive little woman—one of those creatures that have settled every question once and for all beyond reopening, "Wells? No! I draw the line at Wells. He stirs up the dregs. I don't mind the froth, but dregs I—will—not have!" And silence reigned as we stared at the reputation of Wells lying dead on the carpet. When, with the thrill of emotion that a great work communicates, I finished reading "Tono-Bungay," I thought of the smart little woman in the Bayswater drawing-room. I was filled with a holy joy because Wells had stirred up the dregs again, and more violently than ever. I rapturously reflected, "How angry this will make them!" "Them" being the whole innumerable tribe of persons, inane *4 Mar. '09*

4 Mar. '09 or chumpish (this adjective I give to the world), who don't mind froth but won't have dregs. Human nature—you get it pretty complete in "Tono-Bungay," the entire tableau! If you don't like the spectacle of man whole, if you are afraid of humanity, if humanity isn't good enough for you, then you had better look out for squalls in the perusal of "Tono-Bungay." For me, human nature is good enough. I love to bathe deep in it. And of "Tono-Bungay" I will say, with solemn heartiness: "By God! This is a book!"

You will have heard that it is the history of a patent medicine—the nostrum of the title. But the rise and fall of Tono-Bungay and its inventor make only a small part of the book. It is rather the history of the collision of the soul of George Ponderevo (narrator, and nephew of the medicine-man) with his epoch. It is the arraignment of a whole epoch at the bar of the conscience of a man who is intellectually honest and powerfully intellectual. George Ponderevo transgresses most of the current codes, but he also shatters them. The entire system of sanctions tumbles down with a clatter like the fall of a corrugated iron church. I do not know what is left standing, unless it be George Ponderevo. I would not call him a lovable, but he is an admirable, man. He is too ruthless, rude, and bitter to be anything but solitary. His harshness is his fault, his one real fault; and his harshness also marks the point where his attitude towards his environment becomes unscientific. The savagery of his description of the family of Frapp, the little Nonconformist baker, and of the tea-drinkers in the housekeeper's room at Bladesover, somewhat impairs even the astounding force of this, George's first and only novel—not because he exaggerates the offensiveness of the phenomena, but because he unscientifically fails to perceive that these people are just as deserving of compassion as he is himself. He seems to think that, in their deafness to the call of the noble in life, these people are guilty of a crime; whereas they are only guilty of a misfortune. The one other slip that George Ponderevo has made is a slight yielding to the temptation of caricature, out of place in a realistic book. Thus he names a halfpenny paper, "The Daily Decorator," and a journalistic peer, "Lord Boom." Yet the few lines in which he hints at the tactics and the psychology of his Lord Boom are *4 Mar. '09*

4 Mar. '09 masterly. So much for the narrator, whose "I" writes the book. I assume that Wells purposely left these matters uncorrected, as being essential to the completeness of George's self-revelation.

I do not think that any novelist ever more audaciously tried, or failed with more honour, to render in the limits of one book the enormous and confusing complexity of a nation's racial existence. The measure of success attained is marvellous. Complete success was, of course, impossible. But, in the terrific rout, Ponderevo never touches a problem save to grip it firmly. He leaves nothing alone, and everything is handled—handled! His fine detachment, and his sublime common-sense, never desert him in the hour when he judges. Naturally his chief weapon in the collision is just common-sense; it is at the impact of mere common-sense that the current system crumbles. It is simply unanswerable common-sense which will infuriate those who do not like the book. When common-sense rises to the lyric, as it does in the latter half of the tale, you have something formidable. Here Wells has united the daily verifiable actualism of novels like "Love and Mr. Lewisham" and

"Kipps," with the large manner of the paramount synthetic scenes in (what general usage compels me to term) his "scientific romances." In the scientific romance he achieved, by means of parables (I employ the word roughly) a criticism of tendencies and institutions which is on the plane of epic poetry. For example, the criticism of specialization in "The First Men in the Moon," the mighty ridicule of the institution of sovereignty in "When the Sleeper Wakes," and the exquisite blighting of human narrow-mindedness in "The Country of the Blind,"—this last one of the radiant gems of contemporary literature, and printed in the *Strand Magazine!* In "Tono-Bungay" he has achieved the same feat, magnified by ten—or a hundred, without the aid of symbolic artifice. I have used the word "epic," and I insist on it. There are passages toward the close of the book which may fitly be compared with the lyrical freedoms of no matter what epic, and which display an unsurpassable dexterity of hand. Such is the scene in which George deflects his flying-machine so as to avoid Beatrice and her horse by sweeping over them. A new thrill, there, in the sexual vibrations! One thinks of it afterwards. And yet such *4 Mar. '09*

4 Mar. '09 flashes are lost when one contemplates the steady shining of the whole. "Tono-Bungay," to my mind, marks the junction of the two paths which the variety of Wells' gift has enabled him to follow simultaneously, and, at the same time, it is his most distinguished and most powerful book.

I have spoken of the angry and the infuriated. Fury can be hot or cold. Of the cold variety is Claudius Clear's in the *British Weekly*. "Extremely clever," says Claudius Clear. "There is, however, no sign of any new power." But, by way of further praise: "The episodes are carefully selected and put together with skill, and there are few really dull passages." This about the man of whom Maeterlinck has written that he has "the most complete and the most logical imagination of the age." (I think Claudius Clear may have been under the impression that he was reviewing a two-hundred-and-fifty-guinea prize novel, selected by Messrs. Lang and Shorter.) Further, "He writes always from the point of a B.Sc." But the most humorous part of the criticism is this. After stating that Ponderevo acknowledges himself to be a liar, a swindler, a thief, an adulterer, and a murderer, Claudius Clear then proceeds: "He is not in the least ashamed of these things. He explains them away with the utmost facility, and we find him at the age of forty-five, *not unhappy, and successfully engaged in problems of aerial navigation*" (my italics). Oh! candid simplicity of soul! Wells, why did you not bring down the wrath of God, or at least make the adulterer fail in the problems of flight? In quoting a description of the Frapps, Claudius Clear says: "I must earnestly apologize for extracting the following passage." Why? As Claudius Clear gets into his third column his fury turns from cold to hot: "It is impossible for me in these columns to reproduce or to describe the amorous episodes in 'Tono-Bungay.' I cannot copy and I cannot summarize the loathsome tale of George Ponderevo's engagement and marriage and divorce. Nor can I speak of his intrigue with a typist, and of the orgy of lust described at the close of the book . . ." Now, there is not a line in the book that could not be printed in the *British Weekly*. There is not a line which fails in that sober decency which is indispensable to the dignity of a masterpiece. As for George's engagement and marriage, it is precisely typical of *4 Mar. '09*

4 Mar. '09 legions such in England and Scotland. As for the intrigue with a typist, has Claudius Clear never heard of an intrigue with a typist before? In faithfully and decently describing an intrigue with a typist, has one necessarily written a "Justine"? And why "orgy of lust"? Orgy of fiddlestick—if I am not being irreverent! The most correct honeymoon is an orgy of lust; and if it isn't, it ought to be. But some temperaments find a strange joy in using the word "lust." See the infuriating disquisition on "Mrs. Grundy" in "Tono-Bungay." The odd thing is, having regard to the thunders of Claudius Clear, that George Ponderevo is decidedly more chaste than nine men out of ten, and than ninety-nine married men out of every hundred. And the book emanates an austerity and a self-control which are quite conspicuous at the present stage of fiction, and which one would in vain search for amid the veiled concupiscence of at least one author whom Claudius Clear has praised, and, I think, never blamed—at least on that score. I leave him to guess the author.

TCHEHKOFF

ONE of the most noteworthy of recent publications in the way of fiction is Anton Tchehkoff's "The Kiss and Other Stories," translated by Mr. R. E. C. Long and published by Duckworth (6s.). A similar volume, "The Black Monk" (same translator and publisher), was issued some years ago. Tchehkoff lived and made a tremendous name in Russia, and died, and England recked not. He has been translated into French, and I believe that there exists a complete edition of his works in German; but these two volumes are all that we have in English. The thanks of the lettered are due to Mr. Long and to his publishers. Tchehkoff's stories are really remarkable. If anyone of authority stated that they rank him with the fixed stars of Russian fiction—Dostoievsky, Turgeneff, Gogol, and Tolstoy—I should not be ready to contradict. To read them, after even the finest stories of de Maupassant or Murray Gilchrist, is like having a bath after a ball. Their effect is extraordinarily one of ingenuousness. Of course, they are not in the least ingenuous, as a fact, but self-conscious and elaborate to the highest degree. The *18 Mar. '09*

18 Mar. '09 progress of every art is an apparent progress from conventionality to realism. The basis of convention remains, but as the art develops it finds more and more subtle methods fitting life to the convention or the convention to life—whichever you please. Tchehkoff's tales mark a definite new conquest in this long struggle. As you read him you fancy that he must always have been saying to himself: "Life is good enough for me. I won't alter it. I will set it down as it is." Such is the tribute to his success which he forces from you.

He seems to have achieved absolute realism. (But there is no absolute, and one day somebody—probably a Russian—will carry realism further.) His climaxes are never strained; nothing is ever idealized, sentimentalized, etherealized; no part of the truth is left out, no part is exaggerated. There is no cleverness, no startling feat of virtuosity. All appears simple, candid, almost childlike. I could imagine the editor of a popular magazine returning a story of Tchehkoff's with the friendly criticism that it showed promise, and that when he had acquired more skill in hitting the reader exactly between the eyes a deal might be possible. Tchehkoff never hits you between the eyes. But he will, nevertheless leave you on the flat of your back. Beneath the outward simplicity of his work is concealed the most wondrous artifice, the artifice that is embedded deep in nearly all great art. All we English novelists ought to study "The Kiss" and "The Black Monk." They will delight every person of fine taste, but to the artist they are a profound lesson. We have no writer, and we have never had one, nor has France, who could mould the material of life, without distorting it, into such complex forms to such an end of beauty. Read these books, and you will genuinely know something about Russia; you will be drenched in the vast melancholy, savage and wistful, of Russian life; and you will have seen beauty. No tale in "The Kiss" is quite as marvellous as either the first or the last tale in "The Black Monk," perhaps; but both volumes are indispensable to one's full education. I do not exaggerate. I must add that on a reader whose taste is neither highly developed nor capable of high development, the effect of the stories will be similar to their effect on the magazine editor. *18 Mar. '09*

THE SURREY LABOURER

1 Apr. '09 It is a great pleasure to see that Mr. George Bourne's "Memoirs of a Surrey Labourer" (Duckworth) has, after two years, reached the distinction of a cheap edition at half-a-crown. I shall be surprised if this book does not continue to sell for about a hundred years. And yet, also, I am surprised that a cheap edition should have come so soon. The "Memoirs" were very well received on their original publication in 1907; some of the reviews were indeed remarkable in the frankness with which they accepted the work as a masterpiece of portraiture and of sociological observation. But the book had no boom such as Mr. John Lane recently contrived for another very good and not dissimilar book, Mr. Stephen Reynolds' "A Poor Man's House." Mr. Stephen Reynolds was more chattered about by literary London in two months than Mr. George Bourne has been in the eight years which have passed since he published his first book about Frederick Bettesworth, the Surrey labourer in question. Mr. Bourne will owe his popularity in 2009 to the intrinsic excellence of his work, but he owes his popularity in 1909 to the dogged and talkative enthusiasm of a few experts *1 Apr. '09* in the press and in the world, and of his publishers. There have been a handful of persons who were determined to make this exceedingly fine book sell, or perish themselves in the attempt; and it has sold. But not with the help of mandarins. It is not in the least the kind of book to catch the roving eye of a mandarin. It is too proud, too austere, too true, and too tonically cruel to appeal to mandarins. It abounds not at all in quotable passages. Its subtitle is: "A Record of the last year of Frederick Bettesworth." The mandarins who happened to see it no doubt turned to seek the death scene at the close, with thoughts of how quotably Ian Maclaren would have described the death of the old labourer, worn out by honest and ill-paid toil, surrounded by his beloved fields, and so forth and so forth. And Mr. George Bourne's description of his hero's death would no doubt put them right off. I give it in full: "July 25 (Thursday).—Bettesworth died this evening at six o'clock." Oh, Colonel Newcome, sugared tears, golden gates, glimmering panes, passings, pilots, harbour bars —had Mr. George Bourne never heard of you?

1 Apr. '09 I should like to assume that all enlightened and curious readers have already perused this book and its forerunner, "The Bettesworth Book" (Lamley and Co.), of which a cheap edition is soon to be had. But my irritating mania for stopping facts in the street and gazing at them makes it impossible for me to assume any such thing. I am perfectly certain that to about 70 per cent. of you the name of George Bourne means naught. I therefore need not apologize for offering the information that these books are books. They set forth the psychology and the everything-else of the backbone, foundation, and original stock of the English race. They deal with England. Naturally, the sacred name of England will call up in your mind visions of the Carlton Club, Blenheim, Regent Street, Tubes, Selfridge's, theatre stalls, the crowd at Lord's, and the brilliant writers of the *New Age*. And these phenomena are a part of England; but I tell you that they are all only the froth on the surface of Bettesworth the labourer. If you regard this as a cryptic saying, read the two books, and you will see light.

SWINBURNE

ON Good Friday night I was out in the High Street, at the cross-roads, where the warp and the woof of the traffic assault each other under a great glare of lamps. The shops were closed and black, except where a tobacconist kept the tobacconist's bright and everlasting vigil; but above the shops occasional rare windows were illuminated, giving hints—dressing-tables, pictures, gas-globes—of intimate private lives. I don't know why such hints should always seem to me pathetic, saddening; but they do. And beneath them, through the dark defile of shutters, motor-omnibuses roared and swayed and curved, too big for the street, and dwarfing it. And automobiles threaded between them, and bicycles dared the spaces that were left. From afar off there came a flying light, like a shot out of a gun, and it grew into a man perched on a shuddering contrivance that might have been invented by H. G. Wells, and swept perilously into the contending currents, and by miracles emerged untouched, and was gone, driven by the desire of the immortal soul within the man. This strange thing happened again and again. The pavements *22 Apr. '09*

22 Apr. '09 were crowded with hurrying or loitering souls, and the omnibuses and autos were full of them: hundreds passed before the vision every moment. And they were all preoccupied; they nearly all bore the weary, egotistic melancholy that spreads like an infection at the close of a fête day in London; the lights of a motor-omnibus would show the rapt faces of sixteen souls at once in their glass cage, driving the vehicle on by their desires. The policeman and the loafers in the ring of fire made by the public-houses at the cross-roads—even these were grave with the universal affliction of life, and grim with the relentless universal egotism. Lovers walked as though there were no heaven and no earth, but only themselves in space. Nobody but me seemed to guess that the road to Delhi could be as naught to this road, with its dark, fleeing shapes, its shifting beams, its black brick precipices, and its thousand pale, flitting faces of a gloomy and decadent race. As says the Indian proverb, I met ten thousand men on the Putney High Street, and they were all my brothers. But I alone was aware of it. As I stood watching autobus after autobus swing round in a fearful semicircle to begin a new journey, I gazed myself into a mystic comprehension of the significance of what I saw. A few yards beyond where the autobuses turned was a certain house with lighted upper windows, and in that house the greatest lyric versifier that England ever had, and one of the great poets of the whole world and of all the ages, was dying: a name immortal. But nobody looked; nobody seemed to care; I doubt if anyone thought of it. This enormous negligence appeared to me to be fine, to be magnificently human. *22 Apr. '09*

The next day all the shops were open, and hundreds of fatigued assistants were pouring out their exhaustless patience on thousands of urgent and bright women; and flags waved on high, and the gutters were banked with yellow and white flowers, and the air was brisk and the roadways were clean. The very vital spirit of energy seemed to have scattered the breath of life generously, so that all were intoxicated by it in the gay sunshine. He was dead then. The waving posters said it. When Tennyson died I felt less hurt; for I had serious charges to bring against Tennyson, which impaired my affection for him. But I was more shocked. When Tennyson died, everybody knew it,

22 Apr. '09 and imaginatively realized it. Everybody was touched. I was saddened then as much by the contagion of a general grief as by a sorrow of my own. But there was no general grief on Saturday. Swinburne had written for fifty years, and never once moved the nation, save inimically, when "Poems and Ballads" came near to being burnt publicly by the hangman. (By "the nation," I mean newspaper readers. The real nation, busy with the problem of eating, dying, and being born all in one room, has never heard of either Tennyson or Swinburne or George R. Sims.) There are poems of Tennyson, of Wordsworth, even of the speciously recondite Browning, that have entered into the general consciousness. But nothing of Swinburne's! Swinburne had no moral ideas to impart. Swinburne never publicly yearned to meet his Pilot face to face. He never galloped on one of Lord George Sanger's horses from Aix to Ghent. He was interested only in ideal manifestations of beauty and force. Except when he grieved the judicious by the expression of political crudities, he never connected art with any form of morals that the British public could understand. He sang. He sang supremely. And it wasn't enough for the British public. The consequence was that his fame spread out as far as undergraduates, and the tiny mob of undergraduates was the largest mob that ever worried itself about Swinburne. Their shouts showed the high-water mark of his popularity. When one of them wrote in a facetious ecstasy over "Dolores," 22 Apr. '09

But you came, O you procuratores
And ran us all in!

that moment was the crown of Swinburne's career as a popular author. With its incomparable finger on the public pulse the *Daily Mail,* on the day when it announced Swinburne's death, devoted one of its placards to the performances of a lady and a dog on a wrecked liner, and another to the antics of a lunatic with a revolver. The *Daily Mail* knew what it was about. Do not imagine that I am trying to be sardonic about the English race and its organs. Not at all. The English race is all right, though ageing now. The English race has committed no crime in demanding from its poets something that Swinburne could not give. I am merely trying to make clear the exceeding strangeness of the apparition of a poet like Swinburne in a place like England.

22 Apr. '09 Last year I was walking down Putney Hill, and I saw Swinburne for the first and last time. I could see nothing but his face and head. I did not notice those ridiculously short trousers that Putney people invariably mention when mentioning Swinburne. Never have I seen a man's life more clearly written in his eyes and mouth and forehead. The face of a man who had lived with fine, austere, passionate thoughts of his own! By the heavens, it was a noble sight. I have not seen a nobler. Now, I knew by hearsay every crease in his trousers, but nobody had told me that his face was a vision that would never fade from my memory. And nobody, I found afterwards by inquiry, had "noticed anything particular" about his face. I don't mind, either for Swinburne or for Putney. I reflect that if Putney ignored Swinburne, he ignored Putney. And I reflect that there is great stuff in Putney for a poet, and marvel that Swinburne never perceived it and used it. He must have been born English, and in the nineteenth century, by accident. He was misprized while living. That is nothing. What does annoy me is that critics who know better are pandering to the national hypocrisy after his death. In a dozen columns he has been sped into the unknown as "a great Victorian"! Miserable dishonesty! Nobody was ever less Victorian than Swinburne. And then when these critics have to skate over the "Poems and Ballads" episode—thin, cracking ice!—how they repeat delicately the word "sensuous," "sensuous." Out with it, tailorish and craven minds, and say "sensual!" For sensual the book is. It is fine in sensuality, and no talking will ever get you away from that. Villiers de L'Isle Adam once wrote an essay on "Le Sadisme Anglais," and supported it with a translation of a large part of "Anactoria." And even Paris was startled. A rare trick for a supreme genius to play on the country of his birth, enshrining in the topmost heights of its literature a lovely poem that cannot be discussed! . . . Well, Swinburne has got the better of us there. He has simply knocked to pieces the theory that great art is inseparable from the Ten Commandments. His greatest poem was written in honour of a poet whom any English Vigilance Society would have crucified. "Sane" critics will naturally observe, in their quiet manner, that "Anactoria" and similar feats were "so unnecessary." Would it were true! *22 Apr. '09*

THE SEVENPENNIES

29 Apr. '09 SOME time ago a meeting (henceforward historic) took place between Mr. Longman, Mr. Macmillan, Mr. Reginald Smith, Mr. Methuen, and Mr. Hutchinson,* of the one part, and Mr. Bernard Shaw, Mr. Maurice Hewlett, and Mr. Anthony Hope, of the other part. Mr. Longman was the host, and the encounter must have been touching. I would have given a complete set of the works of Mrs. Humphry Ward to have been invisibly present. The publishers had invited the authors (who represented the Authors' Society), with the object of dissuading them from allowing their books to be reprinted at the price of sevenpence. Naturally, the publishers, as always, were actuated by a pure desire for the welfare of authors. Messrs Shaw, Hewlett, and Hope have written an official account of their impressions of the great sevenpenny question, and it appears in the current number of the *Author*. It is amusing. The most amusing aspect of the whole affair is the mere fact that one solitary Scotch firm, Nelsons—

* All baronets or knights now, except Reginald Smith, who is dead.

have forced the mandarins, nay, the arch-mandarins, of the trade to cry out that the shoe is pinching. For the supreme convention of life on the mandarinic plane is that the shoe never pinches. The publishers made one very true statement to the authors, namely, that sevenpenny editions give the public the impression that 6s. is an excessive price for a novel. Well, it is. But is that a reason for abolishing the sevenpenny? The other statements of the publishers were chiefly absurd. For instance, this: "Any author allowing a novel to be sold at sevenpence will find the sales of his next book at 6s. suffering a considerable decrease." Well, it is notorious that if the sevenpenny publishers are publishing one particular book just now, that book is "Kipps." It is equally notorious that the sales of "Tono-Bungay" are, and continue to be, extremely satisfactory. *29 Apr. '09*

On the other hand, the remarks of the sevenpenny publishers themselves are not undiverting. I have heard from dozens of people in the trade that Messrs. Nelson could not possibly make the sevenpenny reprint pay. I have never believed the statement. But the Shaw and Co. report makes Messrs.

29 Apr. '09 Nelson give as one reason for not abandoning the sevenpenny enterprise the fact that "the machinery already in existence is too costly to be abandoned." Which involves the novel maxim that a loss may be too big to be cut! Were their amazing factory ten times as large as it actually is, Messrs. Nelson would have to put it to other uses in face of a regular loss on their sevenpennies. However, there is no doubt in my mind that the enterprise is, and will be, remunerative. The Shaw and Co. report is of the same view. Did the mandarins imagine that they were going to stop the sevenpenny, that anything could stop it? I suppose they did! More agreeably comic than the attitude and arguments of the publishers are the attitude and arguments of the booksellers. But the largest firms, Smith and Son and Wymans, "do not find that the sevenpenny has interfered with the 6s. novel." Be it noted that Smith and Son are now the largest buyers of 6s. novels in England.

In the Shaw and Co. report, in the arguments of publishers, in the arguments of booksellers, not a word about the interests of the consumer! Yet the consumer will settle the affair ultimately. That the price of new novels will come down is absolutely certain. It will come down because it is ridiculous, and no mandarinic efforts can keep it up. In the process of readjustment many people will temporarily suffer, and a few people will be annihilated. But things are what they are, and the consequences of them will be what they will be. Why, therefore, should we deceive ourselves? I quite expect to suffer myself. I shall not, however, complain of the cosmic movement. The auctorial report (which, by the way, is full of common-sense) envisages immense changes in the book-market. I agree. And I am sure that these changes will come about in the teeth of violent opposition from both publishers and booksellers. The book-market is growing steadily. It is enormous compared to what it used to be. And yet it is only in its infancy. The inhabitants of this country have scarcely even begun to buy books. Wait a few years and you will see! *29 Apr. '09*

MEREDITH

27 May '09 THE death of George Meredith removes, not the last of the Victorian novelists, but the first of the modern school. He was almost the first English novelist whose work reflected an intelligent interest in the art which he practised; and he was certainly the first since Scott who was really a literary man. Even Scott was more of an antiquary than a man of letters—apart from his work. Can one think of Dickens as a man of letters, as one who cared for books, as one whose notions on literature were worth twopence? And Thackeray's opinions on contemporary and preceding writers condemn him past hope of forgiveness. Thackeray was in Paris during the most productive years of French fiction, the sublime decade of Balzac, Stendhal, and Victor Hugo. And his Paris sketchbook proves that his attitude towards the marvels by which he was surrounded was the attitude of a clubman. These men wrote; they got through their writing as quickly as they could; and during the rest of the day they were clubmen, or hosts, or guests. Trollope, who dashed off his literary work with a watch in front of him before 8.30 of a morning, who hunted three days a week, dined out enormously, and gave his best hours to fighting Rowland Hill in the Post Office,—Trollope merely carried to its logical conclusion the principle of his mightier rivals. What was the matter with all of them, after a holy fear of their publics, was simple ignorance. George Eliot was not ignorant. Her mind was more distinguished than the minds of the great three. But she was too preoccupied by moral questions to be a first-class creative artist. And she was a woman. A woman, at that epoch, dared not write an entirely honest novel! Nor a man either! Between Fielding and Meredith no entirely honest novel was written by anybody in England. The fear of the public, the lust of popularity, feminine prudery, sentimentalism, Victorian niceness, —one or other of these things prevented honesty. *27 May '09*

In "Richard Feverel," what a loosening of the bonds! What a renaissance! Nobody since Fielding would have ventured to write the Star and Garter chapter in "Richard Feverel." It was the announcer of a sort of dawn. But there are fearful faults in "Richard Feverel." The book is sicklied

27 May '09 o'er with the pale cast of the excellent Charlotte M. Yonge. The large constructional lines of it are bad. The separation of Lucy and Richard is never explained, and cannot be explained. The whole business of Sir Julius is grotesque. And the conclusion is quite arbitrary. It is a weak book, full of episodic power and overloaded with wit. "Diana of the Crossways" is even worse. I am still awaiting from some ardent Meredithian an explanation of Diana's marriage that does not insult my intelligence. Nor is "One of our Conquerors" very good. I read it again recently, and was sad. In my view, "The Egoist" and "Rhoda Fleming" are the best of the novels, and I don't know that I prefer one to the other. The later ought to have been called "Dahlia Fleming," and not "Rhoda." When one thinks of the rich colour, the variety, the breadth, the constant intellectual distinction, the sheer brilliant power of novels such as these, one perceives that a "great Victorian" could only have succeeded in an age when all the arts were at their lowest ebb in England, and the most middling of the middle-classes ruled with the Bible in one hand and the Riot Act in the other.

MEREDITH

Meredith was an uncompromizing Radical, and—what is singular—he remained so in his old age. He called Mr. Joseph Chamberlain's nose 'adventurous' at a time when Mr. Joseph Chamberlain's nose had the ineffable majesty of the Queen of Spain's leg. And the *Pall Mall* haughtily rebuked him. A spectacle for history! He said aloud in a ball-room that Guy de Maupassant was the greatest novelist that ever lived. To think so was not strange; but to say it aloud! No wonder this temperament had to wait for recognition. Well, Meredith has never had proper recognition; and won't have yet. To be appreciated by a handful of writers, gushed over by a little crowd of thoughtful young women, and kept on a shelf uncut by ten thousand persons determined to be in the movement—that is not appreciation. He has not even been appreciated as much as Thomas Hardy, though he is a less fine novelist. I do not assert that he is a less fine writer. For his poems are as superior to the verses of Thomas Hardy as "The Mayor of Casterbridge" is superior to "The Egoist." (Never in English prose literature was such a seer of beauty as Thomas Hardy.) The volume of Meredith's verse is small, but there are things in it that *27 May '09*

27 May '09 one would like to have written. And it is all so fine, so acute, so alert, courageous, and immoderate.

A member of the firm which has the honour of publishing Meredith's novels was interviewed by the *Daily Mail* on the day after his death. The gentleman interviewed gave vent to the usual insolence about our own times. "He belonged," said the gentleman, "to a very different age from the *modern* writer—an age before the literary agent; and with Mr. Meredith the feeling of intimacy as between author and publisher—the feeling that gave to publishing as it was its charm—was always existent." Charm,—yes, for the publisher. The secret history of the publishing of Meredith's earlier books (long before Constables had ever dreamed of publishing him) is more than curious. I have heard some details of it. My only wonder is that human ingenuity did not invent literary agents forty years ago. Then the person interviewed went grandly on: "In his manner of writing the great novelist was very different from the *modern* fashion. He wrote with such care that judged by *modern* standards he would be considered a trifle slow." Tut-tut! It may interest the gentleman interviewed to learn that no modern writer would dare to produce work at the rate at which Scott, Dickens, Trollope and Thackeray produced it when their prices were at their highest. The rate of production has most decidedly declined, and upon the whole novels are written with more care now than ever they were. I should doubt if any novel was written at greater speed than the greatest realistic novel in the world, Richardson's "Clarissa," which is eight or ten times the length of an average novel by Mrs. Humphry Ward. "Mademoiselle de Maupin" was done in six weeks. Scott's careless dash is notorious. And both Dickens and Thackeray were in such a hurry that they would often begin to print before they had finished writing. Publishers who pride themselves on the old charming personal relations with great authors ought not to be so ignorant of literary history as the gentleman who unpacked his heart to a sympathetic *Daily Mail.* *27 May '09*

ST. JOHN HANKIN

1 July '09 I WAS discussing last week the insufficiency of the supply of intelligent playwrights for the presumable demand of the two new repertory theatres; and, almost as I spoke, St. John Hankin drowned himself. The loss is sensible. I do not consider St. John Hankin to have been a great dramatist; I should scarcely care to say that he was a distinguished dramatist, though, of course, the least of his works is infinitely more important in the development of the English theatre than the biggest of the creaking contrivances for which Sir Arthur Wing Pinero has recently received honour from a grateful and cultured Government. But he was a curious, honest, and original dramatist, with a considerable equipment of wit and of skill. The unconsciously grotesque condescension which he received in the criticisms of Mr. William Archer, and the mere insolence which he had to tolerate in the criticisms of Mr. A. B. Walkley, were demonstrations of the fact that he was a genuine writer. What he lacked was creative energy. He could interest but he could not powerfully grip you. His most precious quality—particularly precious in England—

was his calm intellectual curiosity, his perfect absence of fear at the logical consequences of an argument. He would follow an argument anywhere. He was not one of those wretched poltroons who say: "But if I admit *x* to be true, I am doing away with the incentive to righteousness. *Therefore* I shall not admit *x* to be true." There are thousands of these highly educated poltroons between St. Stephen's Westminster and Aberystwith University, and St. John Hankin was their foe. *1 July '09*

The last time I conversed with him was at the dress rehearsal of a comedy. Between the sloppy sounds of charwomen washing the floor of the pit and the feverish cries of photographers taking photographs on the stage, we discussed the plays of Tchekhoff and other things. He was one of the few men in England who had ever heard of Tchekhoff's plays. When I asked him in what edition he had obtained them, he replied that he had read them in manuscript. I have little doubt that one day these plays will be performed in England. St. John Hankin was an exceedingly good talker, rather elaborate in the construction of his phrases, and occasionally dandiacal

1 July '09 in his choice of words. One does not arrive at his skill in conversation without taking thought, and he must have devoted a lot of thought to the art of talking. Hence he talked self-consciously, fully aware all the time that talking was an art and himself an artist. Beneath the somewhat finicking manner there was visible the intelligence that cared for neither conventions nor traditions, nor for possible inconvenient results, but solely for intellectual honesty amid conditions of intellectual freedom.

UNCLEAN BOOKS

THE Rev. Dr. W. F. Barry, himself a novelist, has set about to belabour novelists, and to enliven the end of a dull season, in a highly explosive article concerning "the plague of unclean books, and especially of dangerous fiction." He says: "I never leave my house to journey in any direction, but I am forced to see, and solicited to buy, works flamingly advertised of which the gospel is adultery and the apocalypse the right of suicide." (No! I am not parodying Dr. Barry. I am quoting from his article, which may be read in the *Bookman*. It ought to have appeared in *Punch*.) One naturally asks oneself: "What is the geographical situation of this house of Dr. Barry's, hemmed in by flaming and immoral advertisements and by soliciting sellers of naughtiness?" Dr. Barry probably expects to be taken seriously. But he will never be taken seriously until he descends from purple generalities to the particular naming of names. If he has the courage of his opinions, if he genuinely is concerned for the future of this unfortunate island, he might name a dozen or so of the "myriad volumes which deride self-control, scoff at the God- *8 July '09*

8 July '09 like in man, deny the judgment, and by most potent illustration declare that death ends all." For myself, I am unacquainted with them, and nobody has ever solicited me to buy them. At least he might state *where* one is solicited to buy these shockers. I would go thither at once, just to see. In the course of his article, Dr. Barry lets slip a phrase about "half-empty churches." Of course, these half-empty churches must be laid on the back of somebody, and the novelist's back is always convenient. Hence, no doubt, the article. Dr. Barry seeks for information. He asks: "Will Christian fathers and mothers go on tolerating . . . ," etc., etc. I can oblige him. The answer is, "Yes. They will."

LOVE POETRY

IN every number up to August, I think, the summary of the *English Review* began with "Modern Poetry," a proper and necessary formal recognition of the supremacy of verse. But in the current issue "Modern Poetry" is put after a "study" of the Chancellor of the Exchequer by Max Beerbohm. A trifling change! editorially speaking, perhaps an unavoidable change! And yet it is one of these nothings which are noticed by those who notice such nothings. Among the poets, some of them fairly new discoveries, whom the *English Review* has printed, is "J. Marjoram." I do not know what individuality the name of J. Marjoram conceals, but it is certainly a pseudonym. Some time ago J. Marjoram published a volume of verse entitled "Repose" (Alston Rivers), and now Duckworth has published his "New Poems." The volume is agreeable and provocative. It contains a poem called "Afternoon Tea," which readers of the *English Review* will remember. I do not particularly care for "Afternoon Tea." I find the contrast between the outcry of a deep passion and the chatter of the tea merely melodramatic, *16 Sep. '09*

16 Sep. '09 instead of impressive. And I object to the idiom in which the passion is expressed. For example:

To prove I mean love, I'd burn in Hell.

Or:

You touch the cup
With one slim finger. . . . I'll drink it up,
Though it be blood.

We are all quite certain that the lover would not willingly burn in Hell to prove his love, and that if he drank blood he would be sick. The idiom is outworn. That J. Marjoram should employ it is a sign, among others, that he has not yet quite got over the "devout lover" stage in his mood towards women. He makes a pin say: "She dropped me, pity my despair!" which is in the worst tradition of *Westminster Gazette* "Occ. Verse." He is somewhat too much occupied with this attitudinization before women or the memory of women. It has about as much to do with the reality of sexual companionship as the Lord Mayor's procession has to do with the municipal life of Greater London. Still, J. Marjoram is a genuine poet. In "Fantasy of the Sick Bed," the principal poem in the book, there are some really beautiful passages. I would say to him, and I would say to all young poets, because I feel it deeply: Do not be afraid of your raw material, especially in the relations between men and women. J. Marjoram well and epigrammatically writes: *16 Sep. '09*

Yet who despizeth Love
As little and incomplete
Learns by losing Love
How it was sweet!

True. But, when applied to love with a capital L, and to dropped pins despairing, a little sane realistic disdain will not be amiss, particularly in this isle. I want to see the rise of a new school of love poetry in England. And I believe I shall see it.

TROLLOPE'S METHODS

23 Sep. '09 I AM reminded of Anthony Trollope and a recent article on him, in the *Times,* which was somewhat below the high level of the *Times* literary criticism. Said the *Times:* "Anthony Trollope died in the December of 1882, and in the following year a fatal, perhaps an irreparable, blow to his reputation was struck by the publication of his autobiography." The conceit of a blow which in addition to being fatal is perhaps also irreparable is diverting. But that is not my point. What the *Times* objects to in the Autobiography is the revelation of the clock-work methods by which Trollope wrote his novels. It appears that this horrid secret ought to have been for ever concealed. "Fatal admission!" exclaims the *Times.* Fatal fiddlesticks! Trollope said much more than the *Times* quotes. He confessed that he wrote with a watch in front of him, and obliged himself to produce 250 words every quarter of an hour. And what then? How can the confession affect his reputation? His reputation rests on the value of his novels, and not in the least on the manner in which he chose to write them. And his reputation is secure. Moreover, there is no reason why great literature should not be produced to time, with a watch on the desk. Persons who chatter about the necessity of awaiting inspirational hypersthenia don't know what the business of being an artist is. They have only read about it sentimentally. The whole argument is preposterous, and withal extraordinarily Victorian. And even assuming that the truth *would* deal a fatal blow, etc., is that a reason for hiding it? Another strange sentence is this: "The wonder is, not that Trollope's novels are 'readable,' but that, *being readable, they are yet* so closely packed with that true realism without which any picture of life is lifeless." (My italics.) I ask myself what quality, in the opinion of the *Times* writer, chiefly makes for readableness. *23 Sep. '09*

CHESTERTON AND LUCAS

7 Oct. '09 Two books of essays on the same day from the same firm, "One Day and Another," by E. V. Lucas, and "Tremendous Trifles," by G. K. Chesterton! Messrs. Methuen put the volumes together and advertised them as being "uniform in size and appearance." I do not know why. They are uniform neither in size nor in appearance; but only in price, costing a crown apiece. "Tremendous Trifles" has given me a wholesome shock. Its contents are all reprinted from the *Daily News*. In some ways they are sheer and rank journalism; they are often almost Harmsworthian in their unscrupulous simplifying of the facts of a case, in their crude determination to emphasize one fact at the expense of every other fact. Thus: "No one can understand Paris and its history who does not understand that its fierceness is the balance and justification of its frivolity." So there you are! If you don't accept that you are damned; the Chesterton guillotine has clicked on you. Perhaps I have lived in Paris more years than Mr. Chesterton has lived in it months, but it has not yet happened to me to understand that its fierceness is the balance and justification of its frivolity. Hence I am undone; I no longer exist! Again, of Brussels: "It has none of the things which make good Frenchmen love Paris; it has only the things which make unspeakable Englishmen love it." There are a hundred things in Brussels that I love, and I find Brussels a very agreeable city. Hence I am an unspeakable Englishman. Mr. Chesterton's book is blotched with this particular form of curt arrogance as with a skin complaint. Happily it is only a skin complaint. More serious than a skin complaint is Mr. Chesterton's religious orthodoxy, which crops up at intervals and colours the book. I merely voice the opinion of the intelligent minority (or majority) of Mr. Chesterton's readers when I say that his championship of Christian dogma sticks in my throat. In my opinion, at this time of day it is absolutely impossible for a young man with a first-class intellectual apparatus to accept any form of dogma, and I am therefore forced to the conclusion that Mr. Chesterton has not got a first-class intellectual apparatus. (With an older man, whose central ideas were definitely formed at an earlier epoch, the case might be different.) I will go further and say that it is impossible, in one's private *7 Oct. '09*

7 Oct. '09 thoughts, to think of the accepter of dogma as an intellectual equal. Not all Mr. Chesterton's immense cleverness and charm will ever erase from the minds of his best readers this impression—caused by his mistimed religious dogmatism—that there is something seriously deficient in the very basis of his mind. And what his cleverness and charm cannot do his arrogance and his effrontery assuredly will not do. And yet I said that this book gave me a wholesome shock. Far from deteriorating, Mr. Chesterton is improving. In spite of the awful tediousness of his mannerism of antithetical epigram, he does occasionally write finer epigrams than ever. His imagination is stronger, his fancy more delicate, and his sense of beauty widened. There are things in this book that really are very excellent indeed; things that, if they die, will die hard. For example, the essay: "In Topsy Turvy Land." It is a book which, in the main, strongly makes for righteousness. Its minor defects are scandalous, in a literary sense; its central defect passes the comprehension; the book is journalism, it is anything you like. But I can tell you that it is literature, after all.

CHESTERTON AND LUCAS

7 Oct. '09

If you desire a book entirely free from the exasperating faults of Mr. Chesterton's you will turn to Mr. Lucas's. But Mr. Lucas, too, is a highly mysterious man. On the surface he might be mistaken for a mere cricket enthusiast. Dig down, and you will come, with not too much difficulty, to the simple man of letters. Dig further, and, with somewhat more difficulty, you will come to an agreeably ironic critic of human foibles. Try to dig still further, and you will probably encounter rock. Only here and there in his two novels does Mr. Lucas allow us to glimpse a certain powerful and sardonic harshness in him, indicative of a mind that has seen the world and irrevocably judged it in most of its manifestations. I could believe that Mr. Lucas is an ardent politician, who, however, would not deign to mention his passionately held views save with a pencil on a ballot-paper—if then! It could not have been without intention that he put first in this new book an essay describing the manufacture of a professional criminal. Most of the other essays are exceedingly light in texture. They leave no loophole for criticism, for their accomplishment is always at least as high as their ambition. They are serenely well done.

7 Oct. '09 Immanent in the book is the calm assurance of a man perfectly aware that it will be a passing hard task to get change out of *him!* And even when someone does get change out of him, honour is always saved. In describing a certain over of his own bowling, Mr. Lucas says: "I was conscious of a twinge as I saw his swift glance round the field. He then hit my first ball clean out of it; from my second he made two; from my third another two; the fourth and fifth wanted playing; and the sixth he hit over my head among some distant haymakers." You see; the fourth and fifth wanted playing.

OFFICIAL RECOGNITION OF POETRY

I DID not go to Paris to witness the fêtes in celebration of the fiftieth anniversary of Victor Hugo's "La Légende des Siècles," but I happened to be in Paris while they were afoot. I might have seen one of Hugo's dramas at the Théâter Français, but I avoided this experience, my admiration for Hugo being tempered after the manner of M. André Gide's. M. Gide, asked with a number of other authors to say who was still the greatest modern French poet, replied: "Victor Hugo—alas!" So I chose Brieux instead of Hugo, and saw "La Robe Rouge" at the Français. Brieux is now not only an Academician, but one of the stars of the Français. A bad sign! A bad play, studded with good things, like all Brieux's plays. (The importance attached to Brieux by certain of the elect in England is absurd. Bernard Shaw could simply eat him up—for he belongs to the vegetable kingdom.) A thoroughly bad performance, studded with fine acting! A great popular success! Whenever I go to the Français I tremble at the prospect of a national theatre in England. The Français is hopeless—corrupt, feeble, *14 Oct. '09*

14 Oct. '09 tedious, reactionary, fraudulent, and the laughing-stock of artists. However, we have not got a national theatre yet.

Immediately after its unveiling I gazed in the garden of the Palais Royal at Rodin's statue of Victor Hugo. I thought it rather fine, shadowed on the north and on the south by two famous serpentine trees. Hugo, in a state of nudity, reclines meditating on a pile of rocks. The likeness is good, but you would not guess from the statue that for many years Hugo travelled daily on the top of the Clichy-Odéon omnibus and was never recognized by the public. Heaven knows what he is meditating about! Perhaps about that gushing biography of himself which apparently he penned with his own hand and published under another name! For he was a weird admixture of qualities—like most of us. I could not help meditating, myself, upon the really extraordinary differences between France and England. Imagine a nude statue of Tennyson in St. James's Park! You cannot! But, assuming that some creative wit had contrived to get a nude statue of Tennyson into St. James's Park, imagine the enormous shindy that would occur, the horror-stricken Press of London, the deep pain and resentment of a mighty race! And can you conceive London officially devoting a week to the recognition of the fact that fifty years had elapsed since the publication of a work of poetic genius! Yet I think we know quite as much about poetry in England as they do in France. Still less conceivable is the participation of an English Government in such an anniversary. In Paris last Thursday a French minister stood in front of the Hugo statue and thus began: "The Government of the Republic could not allow the fiftieth anniversary of the 'Legend of the Centuries' to be celebrated without associating itself with the events." My fancy views Mr. Herbert John Gladstone—yes, him!—standing discreetly in front of an indiscreet marble Wordsworth and asserting that the British Government had no intention of being left out of the national rejoicings about the immortality of "The Prelude"! A spectacle that surely Americans would pay to see! On Sunday, at the Français, Hugo was being declaimed from one o'clock in the afternoon till midnight, with only an hour's interval. And it rained violently nearly all the time. *14 Oct. '09*

ARTISTS AND CRITICS

21 Oct. '09 THERE is a one-sided feud between artists and critics. When a number of artists are gathered together you will soon in the conversation come upon signs of that feud. I admit that the general attitude of artists to critics is unfair. They expect from critics an imaginative comprehension which in the nature of the case only a creative artist can possess. On the other hand, a creative artist cannot do the work of a critic because he has neither the time nor the inclination to master the necessary critical apparatus. Hence critical work seldom or never satisfies the artist, and the artist's ideal of what critical work ought to be is an impossible dream. I find confirmation of my view in other arts than my own. The critical work of Mr. Bernhard Berenson, for instance, seems to me wonderful and satisfying. But when I mention Mr. Berenson to a painter I invariably discover that that painter's secret attitude towards Mr. Berenson is—well, aristocratic. The finest, and the only first-rate, criticism is produced when, by an exceptional accident, a creative artist of balanced and powerful temperament is moved to deal exhaustively with a subject.

ARTISTS AND CRITICS

Among standard critical works the one that has most impressed me is Lessing's "Laocoon"—at any rate the literary parts of it. Here (I have joyously said to myself) is somebody who knows what he is talking about. Here is someone who has *been there.* *21 Oct. '09*

RUDYARD KIPLING

4 Nov. '09 AFTER a long period of abstention from Rudyard Kipling, I have just read "Actions and Reactions." It has induced gloom in me; yet a modified gloom. Nearly a quarter of a century has passed since "Plain Tales from the Hills" delighted first Anglo-Indian, and then English society. There was nothing of permanent value in that book, and in my extremest youth I never imagined otherwise. But "The Story of the Gadsbys" impressed me. So did "Barrack-room Ballads." So did pieces of "Soldiers Three." So did "Life's Handicap" and "Many Inventions." So did "The Jungle Book," despite its wild natural history. And I remember my eagerness for the publication of "The Seven Seas." I remember going early in the morning to Denny's bookshop to buy it. I remember the crimson piles of it in every bookshop in London. And I remember that I perused it, gulped it down, with deep joy. And I remember the personal anxiety which I felt when Kipling lay very dangerously ill in New York. For a fortnight, then, Kipling's temperature was the most important news of the day. I remember giving a party with a programme of music, in that fortnight, and I began the proceedings by reading aloud the programme, and at the end of the programme instead of "God Save the Queen," I read, "God Save Kipling," and everybody cheered. "Stalky and Co." cooled me and "Kim" chilled me. At intervals, since, Kipling's astounding political manifestations, chiefly in verse, have shocked and angered me. As time has elapsed it has become more and more clear that his output was sharply divided into two parts by his visit to New York, and that the second half is inferior in quantity, in quality, in everything, to the first. It has been too plain now for years that he is against progress, that he is the shrill champion of things that are rightly doomed, that his vogue among the hordes of the respectable was due to political reasons, and that he retains his authority over the said hordes because he is the bard of their prejudices and of their clayey ideals. A democrat of ten times Kipling's gift and power could never have charmed and held the governing classes as Kipling has done. Nevertheless, I for one cannot, except in anger, go back on a genuine admiration. I cannot forget a benefit. If in quick resentment I have ever *4 Nov. '09*

4 Nov. '09 written of Kipling with less than the respect which is eternally due to an artist who has once excited in the heart a generous and beautiful emotion, and has remained honest, I regret it. And this is to be said: at his worst Kipling is an honest and painstaking artist. No work of his but has obviously been lingered over with a craftsman's devotion! He has never spoken when he had nothing to say—though probably no artist was ever more seductively tempted by publishers and editors to do so. And he has done more than shun notoriety—Miss Marie Corelli does that—he has succeeded in avoiding it.

The first story, and the best, in "Actions and Reactions," is entitled "An Habitation Enforced," and it displays the amused but genuine awe of a couple of decent rich Americans confronted by the sæcular wonders of the English land system. It depends for its sharp point on a terrific coincidence, as do many of Kipling's tales, for instance, "The Man Who Was," the mere chance that these Americans should tumble upon the very ground and estate that had belonged to the English ancestors of one of them. It is written in a curiously tortured idiom, largely borrowed from the Bible, and all the characters are continually given to verbal smartness or peculiarity of one kind or another. The characters are not individualized. Each is a type, smoothed out by sentimental handling into something meant to be sympathetic. Moreover, the real difficulties of the narrative are consistently, though I believe unconsciously, shirked. The result, if speciously pretty, is not a bit convincing. But the gravest, and the entirely fatal fault, is the painting of the English land system. To read this story one could never guess that the English land system is not absolutely ideal, that tenants and hereditary owners do not live always in a delightful patriarchal relation, content. There are no shadows whatever. The English land system is perfect, and no accusation could possibly be breathed against it. And the worst is that for Kipling the English land system probably *is* perfect. He is incapable of perceiving that it can be otherwise. He would not desire it to be otherwise. His sentimentalization of it is gross—there is no other word—and at bottom the story is as wildly untrue to life as the most arrant Sunday-school prize ever published by the Religious Tract Society. Let it be admitted *4 Nov. '09*

4 Nov. '09 that the romantic, fine side of the English land system is rendered with distinction and effectiveness; and that the puzzled, unwilling admiration of the Americans is well done, though less well than in a somewhat similar earlier story, "An Error in the Fourth Dimension."

An example of another familiar aspect of Kipling is "With the Night Mail." This is a story of 2000 A.D., and describes the crossing of the Atlantic by the aerial mail. It is a glittering essay in the sham-technical; and real imagination, together with a tremendous play of fancy, is shown in the invention of illustrative detail. But the whole effort is centred on the mechanics of the affair. Human evolution has stood stock-still save in the department of engineering. The men are exactly the same semi-divine civil service men that sit equal with British military and naval officers on the highest throne in the kingdom of Kipling's esteem. Nothing interests him but the mechanics and the bureaucratic organization and the *esprit de corps*. Nor does he conceive that the current psychology of ruling and managing the earth will ever be modified. His simplicity, his naïveté, his enthusiasms, his prejudices, his blindness, and his vanities are those of Stalky. And, after all, even the effect he aims at is not got. It is nearly got, but never quite. There is a tireless effort, but the effort is too plain and fatigues the reader, forcing him to share it. A thin powder of dullness lies everywhere. *4 Nov. '09*

When I had read these stories, I took out "Life's Handicap," and tasted again the flavour of "On Greenhow Hill," which I have always considered to be among the very best of Kipling's stories. It would be too much to say that I liked it as well as ever. I did not. Time has staled it. The author's constitutional sentimentality has corroded it in parts. But it is still a very impressive and a fundamentally true thing. It was done in the rich flush of power, long before its creator had even suspected his hidden weaknesses, long before his implacable limitations had begun to compel him to imitate himself. It was done in the days when he could throw off exquisite jewels like this, to deck the tale:

To Love's low voice she lent a careless ear;
Her hand within his rosy fingers lay,

4 Nov. '09 *A chilling weight. She would not turn or hear;*
But with averted face went on her way.
But when pale Death, all featureless and grim,
Lifted his bony hand, and beckoning
Held out his cypress-wreath, she followed him,
And Love was left forlorn and wondering,
That she who for his bidding would not stay,
At Death's first whisper rose and went away.

CENSORSHIP BY THE LIBRARIES

THE immediate origin of the new attempt by the libraries to exercise a censorship over books, and particularly over novels, is quite accidental and silly. A woman socially prominent in the governing classes of this realm has a daughter. The daughter obtained and read a certain book from the circulating library. (Naturally the family is one of those that are too rich to buy books; it can only hire.) The mother chanced to see the book, and considered it to be highly improper. (I have not read the book, but I should say that it is probably not improper at all; merely a trivial, foolish book.) The woman went direct to an extremely exalted member of the Cabinet, being a friend of his; and she kicked up a tremendous storm and dust. The result was that "certain machinery" was set in motion, and "certain representations" were made to the libraries; indeed, the libraries were given to understand that unless they did something themselves "certain steps" would be taken. It was all very vague and impressive, and it brought recent agitations to a head. Hence the manifesto of the *23 Dec. '09*

23 Dec. '09 libraries, in which they announce that all books must be submitted in advance to a committee of hiring experts, and that the submitted books will be divided into three classes. The first class will be absolutely banned; the circulation of the second will be prevented so far as it can be prevented without the ban absolute; and the circulation of the third will be permitted without restrictions.

Of course, that even the suggestion of a censorship should spring from such a personal and trifling cause is very scandalous. But I am fairly sure that it might happen under any Government and under any form of Government. All Governments must consist of individual members, and all individual members have friends. Most of them are acquainted with women, and with absurd women, who will utilize the acquaintanceship with all their might for their own personal ends. And exceedingly few members of any Government whatsoever would have the courage to tell a well-dressed and arrogant woman to go to the devil, even when that answer happened to be the sole correct answer to an impertinence. Wellington merely damned the portly darlings, but then Wellington, though preposterous as a politician, was a great man. *23 Dec. '09*

The menacing letter from the Libraries was received by the Publishers on the very day of their Council meeting. This may or may not have been accidental, but at any rate it put the Publishers at a disadvantage. The Council meetings of the Publishers' Association, being dominated by knights and other mandarins, are apt to be formal and majestic in character. You can't blurt out whatever comes into your head at a Council meeting of the Publishers' Association. And nearly everybody is afraid of everybody else. No one had had time to think the matter over, much less to decide whether surrender or defiance would pay best or look best. Consequently the reply sent to the Libraries was a masterpiece of futility. The mildly surprising thing is that, in the Council itself, there was a strong pro-Library party. Among this party were Messrs. Hutchinson and Mr. Heinemann. Messrs. Hutchinson, it is well known, have consistently for many years tried to publish only novels for "family reading." It is an ambition, like another. And one may admit that Messrs. Hutchinson have fairly well

23 Dec. '09 succeeded in it. Mr. Heinemann issues as much really high-class literature as any publisher in London, but if his policy has had a "family and young lady" tendency, that tendency has escaped me. He has published books (some of them admirable works, and some not) which a committee of hiring experts would have rejected with unanimous enthusiasm. It is needless to particularize. Why Mr. Heinemann should have supported the Libraries in the private deliberations of the Publishers I cannot imagine. But that is the fault of my imagination. I have an immense confidence in Mr. Heinemann's business acumen and instinct for self-preservation.

The Publishers, if they chose, could kill the censorship movement at once by politely declining to submit their books to the censorship. If only the three big fiction firms concerted to do this, the Libraries would be compelled to withdraw their project. But the Publishers will not do this; not even three of them will do it. The only argument against a censorship is that it is extremely harmful to original literature of permanent value; and such an argument does not make any very powerful appeal to publishers. What most publishers want is to earn as much money as possible with as little fuss as possible. Again, the Authors' Society might kill the censorship conspiracy by declining to allow its members to sign any agreement with publishers which did not contain a clause forbidding the publisher to submit the book to the committee of hiring experts. A dozen leading novelists could command the situation. But the Authors' Society will do nothing effective. The official reply of the Authors' Society was as feeble as that of the Publishers. I repeat that the only argument against a censorship is that it is extremely harmful to original literature of permanent value; such an argument does not make any very powerful appeal to authors. What most authors want is to earn as much money as possible with as little fuss as possible. Besides, the great money-makers among authors—the authors of weight with publishers and libraries—have nothing to fear from any censorship. They censor themselves. They take the most particular care not to write anything original, courageous, or true, because these qualities alienate more subscribers than they please. I am not a pessimist nor a cynic, but I enjoy contemplating the real facts of a case.

23 Dec. '09

23 Dec. '09 All the forces would seem to be in favour of the establishment of a censorship. (And by a censorship I mean such a censorship as would judge books by a code which, if it was applied to them, would excommunicate the Bible, Shakespeare, Defoe, Richardson, Fielding, Sterne, Swift, Shelley, Rossetti. Meredith, Hardy, and George Moore. "The Ordeal of Richard Feverel" would never, as a new work, pass a library censorship. Nor would "Jude the Obscure," nor half a dozen of Hardy's other books; nor would most of George Moore.) Nevertheless I am not very much perturbed. There are three tremendous forces against the establishment of a genuine censorship, and I think that they will triumph. The first is that mysterious nullifying force by which such movements usually do fizzle out. The second force against it lies in the fact that the movement is not genuinely based on public opinion. And the third is that there is a great deal of money to be made out of merely silly mawkish books which a genuine censorship would ban with serious, original work. For such books a strong demand exists among people otherwise strictly respectable, far stronger than the feeling against such books. The demand will have its way.

CENSORSHIP BY THE LIBRARIES

A few serious and obstinate authors will perhaps suffer for awhile. But then we often do suffer. We don't seem to mind. No one could guess, for instance, from the sweet Christian kindliness of my general tone towards Mr. Jesse Boot's library that Mr. Jesse Boot had been guilty of banning some of my work which I love most. But it is so. I suppose we don't mind, because in the end dead or alive we come out on top. *23 Dec. '09*

I imagined that I had said the last word on this subject, and hence I intended to say no more. But it appears that I was mistaken. It appears, from a somewhat truculent letter which I have received from a correspondent, that I have not yet even touched the fringe of the subject. Parts of this correspondent's letter are fairly printable. He says: "You look at the matter from quite the wrong point of view. There is only one point of view, and that is the subscribers'. The Libraries don't exist for authors, but for us (he is a subscriber to Mudie's). We pay, and the Libraries are for our convenience. They are not for the furtherance of English literature, or whatever you call it. What I say is, if I order a *30 Dec. '09*

30 Dec. '09 book from a Library I ought to be able to get it, unless it has been confiscated by the police. I didn't pay my subscription in order to have my choice of books limited to such books as some frock-coated personage in Oxford Street thought good for me. I've spent about forty years in learning to know what I like in literature, and I don't want anybody to teach me. I'm not a young girl, I'm a middle-aged man; but I don't see why I should be handicapped by that. And if I am to be handicapped I'm going to chuck Mudie's. I've already written them a very rude letter about Mr. de Morgan's "It Never Can Happen Again." I wanted that book. They told me they didn't supply it. And when I made a row they wrote me a soothing letter nearly as long as the Epistle to the Ephesians explaining why they didn't supply it. Something about two volumes and a half-a-sovereign. . . . I don't know, and I don't care. I don't care whether a book's in one volume or in a hundred volumes. If I want it, and if I've paid for the right to have it, I've got to have it, or I've got to have my money back. They mumbled something in their letter about having received many complaints from other subscribers about novels being in two volumes. But what do I care about other subscribers?" *30 Dec. '09*

And he continues, after a deviation into forceful abuse: "I don't want to force novels in two volumes down the throats of other subscribers. I don't want to force anything down their throats. They aren't obliged to take what they don't want. There are lots of books circulated by Mudie's that I strongly object to—books that make me furious—as regards both moral and physical heaviness and tediousness and general tommy-rot. But do I write and complain, and ask Mudie's to withdraw such books altogether? If Mudie's came along with a pistol and two volumes by Hall Caine, and said to me, 'Look here, I'll make you have these,' then perhaps I might begin to murmur gently. But he doesn't. I'll say this for Mudie; he doesn't force you to take particular books. You can always leave what you don't want. All these people who are (alleged to be) crying out for a censorship,—they're merely idle! If they really want a censorship they ought to exercise it themselves. Robinson has a daughter, and he is shocked at the idea of her picking up a silly sham-erotic novel by a

30 Dec. '09 member of the aristocracy, or a first-rate beautiful thing by George Moore. . . . Am I then to be deprived of the chance of studying the inane psychology of the ruling classes or of enjoying the work of a great artist? Be d——d to Robinson's daughter! I don't care a bilberry for either her or her innocence. I'm not going to be responsible for Robinson's daughter. Let Robinson, if he is such a fool as to suppose that daughters can be spoiled by bad books or good books—let him look after her himself! Let him establish his confounded censorship at his front door, or at his drawing-room door. Let him do his own work. Nothing but idleness—that's what's the matter with him! The whole project that Robinson suggests is simply monstrous. He might just as well say that because his daughter has a weak digestion and an unruly appetite for rich cakes, therefore all the cake shops in London must be shut up. Let him keep her out of cake shops. All I want is freedom. I don't mean to defend my tastes or to apologize for them. If I wish to hire a certain book, that's enough. I must have it—until the police step in. There can only be one censorship, and that is by the police. A Library is a commercial concern, and I won't look at it from any other point of view. I have no interest at the present moment in your emotions about the future of literature, and the livelihood of serious artists, and so on. All that's absolutely beside the point. The sole point is that I am ready to let other people have what they want, and I claim that I've the right to have what I want. The whole thing is simple rot, and there's no other word for it." *30 Dec. '09*

1910

CENSORSHIP BY THE LIBRARIES

A NUMBER of people have been good enough to explain to me that the project of the Circulating Libraries Censorship (now partially "in being") did not originally concern itself with novels, and that, in the first place, it was directed against books of more or less scandalous memoirs. Of this I was well aware. But in writing about the matter I expressly tried to centre its interest on the novel, because the novel is the only important part of the affair. For a year past I have been inveighing against the increasing taste for feeble naughtiness concerning king's mistresses and all that sort of tedious person. And I have remarked on the growing frequency of such words as "fair," "frail," "lover," "enchantress," etc., in the supposed-to-be-alluring titles of books of historical immorality. (I presume that these volumes are called for by the respectable, as the cocotte calls for a *crême de menthe* at a fashionable seaside hotel on a winter Sunday afternoon.) Apparently the circulating libraries also have noticed the growing frequency of such words in their lists. But what they have noticed with more genuine *13 Jan. '10*

13 Jan. '10 alarm is the growing prices which clever publishers have been putting on such books. It has not escaped the observation of clever publishers that the demand by library subscribers for such books is a very real demand, and clever publishers therefore thought that they might make a little bit extra in this connexion by charging high for volumes brief but scandalous. The libraries thought otherwise. Hence, in truth, the attempted censorship. The now famous moral crusade of the libraries would certainly not have occurred had not the libraries perceived, in the moral pressure which was exercised upon them from lofty regions, the chance of effecting economies. And there is not a circulating library that does not feel an authentic need of economies.

I should have objected to a censorship even of scandalized history, for no censorship ever cured a population of bad taste. But naturally the libraries could not stop at memoirs. They had, in order to be consistent and to talk big about morality, to include novels in their scheme of scavenging. At this point the libraries pass from futile foolishness to active viciousness, and so encounter the opposition of persons like myself, whose business it is to keep an eye on things. *13 Jan. '10*

I can tell a true tale about one of the three great circulating libraries. A certain man of taste was directing the education in literature of a certain woman. The time came when the woman had to study Balzac. The man gave her a list of titles of novels by Balzac which she was to read. She went to her library, but could not find, in the list of Balzac's complete "Comédie Humaine" furnished by the library, one of the works which she had been instructed to peruse. Hearing of this, the man, whose curiosity was aroused, called at the library to conduct an inquiry. He had an interview with one of the managers, and the manager at once admitted that their complete list was not complete. "We cannot supply a work with such a title," the manager explained. The book was one of the most famous and one of the finest of nineteenth-century novels, "Splendeurs et Misères de Courtisanes," issued by Messrs. Dent and Co. (surely a respectable firm), with a preface by Professor George Saintsbury (surely a respectable mandarin), under the title, "The Harlot's Progress." The man of taste

13 Jan. '10 asked, "Have you read the book?" "No," said the manager. "Have you read any of Balzac's novels?" "No," said the manager. "Do you prohibit Galsworthy's 'Man of Property'?" "No," said the manager. "Have you read it?" "No," said the manager. "Do you prohibit Jacob Tonson's last novel?" "No," said the manager. "Have you read it?" "No," said the manager. "Well," said the man of taste, "you'd better read one or two of these later writers, and then think over the Balzac question." The manager discreetly replied that he would consult the principal proprietor. The next morning "The Harlot's Progress," in two volumes, was sent round from the library.

But imagine it! Imagine one of the largest circulating libraries in the world, in the year 1909, refusing to supply an established, world-admired, classical work of genius because its title contains the word "harlot"! In no other European capital, nor in any American capital, could such a monstrously idiotic and disgusting thing happen. It is so preposterous that one cannot realize it all at once. I am a tremendous admirer of England. I have lived too long in foreign parts not to see the fineness of England. But in matters of hypocrisy there is really something very wrong with this island, and the atmosphere of this island is thick enough to choke all artists dead. You can walk up and down the Strand and see photographs of celebrated living harlots all over the place. You can buy them on picture postcards for your daughter. You can see their names even on the posters of high-class weekly papers. You can entertain them at the most select fashionable restaurants. Indeed, the shareholders of fashionable restaurants would look very blue without the said harlots. (Only they aren't called harlots.) But if you desire to read a masterpiece of social fiction, some mirror of crass stupidity in a circulating library will try to save you from yourself. *13 Jan. '10*

Up Yorkshire way the opponents of freedom have been dealing some effective blows at the Libraries Censorship. They doubtless imagine that they have been supporting the Libraries Censorship; but they are mistaken. Hull has distinguished itself. It is a strange, interesting place. I only set foot in it once; the day was Sunday, and I *24 Feb. '10*

24 Feb. '10 arrived by sea. I was informed that a man could not get a shave in Hull on Sunday. But I got one. At the last meeting of the Hull Libraries Committee, when "Ann Veronica" was under discussion, Canon Lambert procured for the name of Lambert a free advertisement throughout the length and breadth of the country by saying: "I would just as soon send a daughter of mine to a house infected with diphtheria or typhoid fever as put that book into her hands." I doubt it. I can conceive that, if it came to the point, Canon Lambert's fear of infection and regard for his own canonical skin might move him to offer his daughter "Ann Veronica" in preference to diphtheria and typhoid fever. Canons who give expression to this kind of babblement must expect what they get in the way of responses. Let the Canon now turn the other cheek, in a Christian spirit, and I will see what I can do for him.

Needless to say, "Ann Veronica" was banned from the Free Public Libraries of free Hull. But I cull the following from the *Hull Daily Mail*: "A local bookseller had thirteen orders for 'Ann Veronica' on Monday, thirty on Tuesday, and scores since. Previously he had no demand." A Canon Lambert in every town would demolish the censorship in less time than it took the Hebrew deity to create the world and the fig-tree. *24 Feb. '10*

Canon Lambert, doubtless unconsciously, went wide of the point. The point was not a code for the parental treatment of canons' daughters. England was not waiting for information as to what Canon Lambert would do to a Miss Lambert in a given dilemma. H. G. Wells did not turn up in Hull with a Gatling gun and, turning it on the Canon's abode, threaten to blow the ecclesiastical wigwam to pieces if the canon did not immediately buy a copy of "Ann Veronica" for his daughter to read. Nobody wants to interfere between the Canon and a Miss Lambert. All that quiet people want is to be left alone to treat their daughters according to their lights. Does Canon Lambert hold that the Hull libraries are to contain no volumes which he would not care for his daughter to read?

The *Hull Daily Mail* has, I regret to say, taken the side of the Canon. This is a pity. The Hull paper should be a little more

24 Feb. '10 careful about the letters it prints. In a recent issue it allowed a correspondent to call "Ann Veronica" "pornographic," which is most distinctly libellous. But possibly the correspondent and the newspaper felt themselves secure in Mr. Wells's disdain. "Ann Veronica" is not pornographic. It is not even indecent. It is utterly decent from end to end. It is also utterly honest. It is not one Mr. Wells's major productions. But if a work of an honourable and honoured artist is to be damned because it happens to be inferior to other works of the same artist, Hull ought to consider the awful case of "Measure for Measure." By the way, would Canon Lambert as soon send a Miss Lambert to a house infected with mumps as put "Measure for Measure" into her hands? The *Hull Daily Mail,* taken to task, sheltered itself behind Mr. Clement Shorter and the *Sphere.* I will not discuss Mr. Shorter's singular pronouncement upon "Ann Veronica," because I am in a very good humour with him just now for his excellently acid remarks upon the "success" literature of Mr. Peter Keary. But I may remark that Mr. Shorter did not advocate the censoring of the book, nor did he come within seven Irish miles of describing it as pornographic. *24 Feb. '10*

Canonical people have tried to make capital out of the fact that "Ann Veronica" is not to be found in the public libraries of sundry large towns. But the reason may not be connected with the iconoclasm of "Ann Veronica." In an interview, Mr. T. W. Hand, the librarian at Leeds, said: "I haven't read the book through (Why not?), though I have seen it, and we haven't got it in any of our libraries in Leeds. The reason for this is not the character of the book, but the fact that we never purchase our novels until they have become cheaper." Charming confession! A subscription ought to be opened for poverty-stricken Leeds, which must wait to buy an English book that is or will be translated into every European language, until it has become cheaper! A few weeks ago the country was laughing at little Beverley because its Fathers publicly decided to purchase no fiction less than a year old. But are the great towns any better off?

Literary censorship in the intellectual centre of the world: I need hardly say that *3 Mar. '10*

3 Mar. '10 I mean Boston, Mass. Boston is the city of Harvard University. It is also the city of the "Atlantic Monthly." It is also the city of Emerson, Lowell, Longfellow, and Holmes. Boston has a Public Library. It is supposed to be one of the finest public libraries in this world or any other. Great artists, such as Puvis de Chavannes and John Sargent, have helped to decorate the Boston Library. In brief, Boston and its Library are not to be sneezed at. A certain woman asked for George Moore's "Esther Waters," recognized, I believe, as one of the most serious and superb of modern novels. The work was included in the catalogue of the Library. In reply to her request she was informed that she could not have "Esther Waters" unless she obtained from the Chief Mandarin or Librarian special permission to read it, on the ground that she was a "student of literature." I doubt whether the imagination of nincompoops and boards of management has ever devised anything more beautiful than this.

But the lady had a husband, and the husband, being a prominent journalist, had the editorial use of a newspaper in Boston. He began to make enquiries, and he discovered that many of the catalogue cards were marked with red stars, and that a star signified that the work described on the card was not morally fit for general circulation. He further discovered that works rankly and frankly pornographic and works of distinguished art were starred with the same star. Lastly, he discovered that the Chief Mandarin or Librarian, all out of his own head and off his own bat, had appointed a reading committee for the dividing of modern fiction into sheep and goats, and that the said committee consisted exclusively of Boston dames mature in years. He exposed the entire affair in his newspapers and made a very pleasing sensation. The first result was that his wife was afterwards received at the Library with imperial honours and given to understand by kowtowing sub-mandarins that she might have the whole red-star library sent home to her house if she so desired. There was no other result. The rest of reading Boston remained under the motherly but autocratic care of *ces dames*. Those skilled in the artistic records of Boston may remember that the management of the same Library once refused the offered gift of a statue of a woman holding a baby, on *3 Mar. '10*

3 Mar. '10 the sole ground that the woman was not attired.

26 May '10 More interesting information has accrued to me concerning literary censorship in the British provinces. Glasgow has about a dozen lending libraries, chiefly, I believe, of the Carnegie species. In none of these are the works of Richardson, Fielding, and Smollett allowed a place. Further, "Anna Karenina," "Resurrection," "Tess," "Jude the Obscure," and "Tono-Bungay" are banned. Further, and still more droll, in the words of a correspondent who has been good enough to send me all sorts of particulars:—"A few days ago I applied at the Mitchell Library (a reference library in the centre of the town) for Whitman's poems. The attendant procured the volume, but, before handing it to me, consulted one of the senior librarians. This official scrutinized me from a distance of about eight yards and finally nodded his head in acquiescence. The book was then given to me. On the back of it a little red label was affixed. I made enquiry and discovered that books with these labels are only given out to persons of (what shall I say?) good moral appearance."

Nevertheless, we ought to be thankful that we live in Britain. The case of the United States is in some respects far worse than ours. The egregious Sir Robert Anderson has just explained in *Blackwood* how he established a sort of unofficial censorship of morals at the English Post Office. In the United States an official censorship of mailed matter exists, and the United States Post Office can and does regularly examine the literature entrusted to it, and can and does reject what it deems inimical to the morals of the native land of Jay Gould, James Gordon Bennett, J. D. Rockefeller, and the regretted Harriman. Among other matter which the United States Post Office censorship has recently excluded are the following items:— *26 May '10*

An extract from an article in the *Fortnightly Review.*

An extract from "Man and Superman."

An article in favour of freedom of the Press reprinted from the Boston's *Woman's Journal.*

An article by Lady Florence Dixie reprinted from a Scottish county paper.

On one occasion the editor of *Lucifer* had occasion to mention that adultery and

26 May '10 fornication had not been criminal offences in England since 1660. The authorities were so aghast at the idea of this information being allowed to creep out that they insisted on the passage being deleted. It was.

Further. The Editor of an American paper, on it being suggested to him that he should reprint portions of a criticism of "Measure for Measure," by Mr. A. B. Walkley in the *Times,* refused to do so for fear of prosecution. Perhaps the most truly American instance of all is the misfortune that befell the Reverend Mabel McCoy Irwin. The excellent lady began to publish a paper advocating strict chastity for both sexes. It was excluded from the mails on the ground that no allusion to sex could be tolerated. I reckon this anecdote to be the most exquisitely perfect of all anecdotes that I have ever come across in the diverting history of moral censorships. There is a subtle flavour about that name, Mabel McCoy Irwin, which is indescribably apposite . . . McCoy. It is a wonderful world! I am much indebted to an American correspondent for these delights.

BRIEUX

I FORESEE a craze in this country for Brieux. I first perceived its coming one day during an intellectual meal in a green-painted little restaurant in Soho. Whenever I go into Soho I pass through experiences which send me out again a wiser man. On this occasion I happened to speak lightly of Brieux to a friend of mine, a prominent and influential member of the Stage Society—one of those men in London who think to-day what London will think to-morrow, and what Paris thought yesterday. He was visibly shocked by my tone. His invincible politeness withstood the strain, but the strain was terrible. From this incident alone I was almost ready to prophesy a Brieux craze in London. And now a selection of Brieux's plays is to be published in English in one volume, with a preface by Bernard Shaw. Within a fortnight of the appearance of the book the Brieux craze will exist in full magnificence. Leading articles will contain learned offhand allusions to Brieux, Brieux and Shaw will be compared and differentiated, and Brieux will be the most serious dramatist in France. I doubt not that Mr. Shaw's preface will be a witty *17 Feb. '10*

17 Feb. '10 and illuminating affair, and that it will show me agreeable aspects of Brieux's talent which have hitherto escaped me; but if it persuades me that Brieux is an artistically serious dramatist worth twopence, then I will retire from public life and seek a post as third sub-editor on the *British Weekly*.

Brieux is a man with moral ideas. I will admit even that he is dominated by moral ideas, which, if they are sometimes crude, are certainly righteous. He is a reformer and a passionate reformer. But a man can be a passionate reformer, with a marked turn for eloquence, and yet not be a serious dramatist. Dr. Clifford is a reformer. Mr. Henniker Heaton is a passionate reformer; and both are capable of literature when they are excited. But they are not dramatists. We still await Mr. Henniker Heaton's tragic fourth act about the failure of the negotiations for a penny post with France. Brieux is too violent a reformer ever to be a serious dramatist. Violent reformers are unprincipled, and the reformer in Brieux forces the dramatist in him to prostitution. The dramatist in him is not strong enough to resist the odious demands of the reformer: which fact alone shows how far he is from being a first-rate dramatist. As a dramatist Brieux is no stronger, no more sincere, no less unscrupulous, no less viciously sentimental, than the fashionable authors of the boulevard, such as Capus, Donnay, and the ineffable Bernstein, so adored in London. And it is as a dramatist that he must be judged. Of course, if you wish to judge him as a reformer, you must get some expert opinion about his subjects of reform. I fancy that you will end by discovering that as a reformer he must be considered just a little crude. *17 Feb. '10*

I have seen most of Brieux's plays, and I have seen them produced under his own direction, so that I can judge fairly well what he is after on the stage. And I am bound to say that, with the exception of "Les Trois Filles de Monsieur Dupont" (which pleased me pretty well so far as I comprehended its dramatic intention), I have not seen one which I could refrain from despising. Brieux's plays always begin so brilliantly, and they always end so feebly, in such a wishwash of sentimentalism. Take his last play—no, his last play was "La Foi," produced by Mr. Tree, and I have not yet met even an ardent disciple of the craze

17 Feb. '10 who has had sufficient effrontery to argue that it is a good play. Take his last play but one, "Suzette"—or "Suzanne," or whatever its girl's name was—produced at the Paris Vaudeville last autumn. The first act is very taking indeed. You can see the situation of the ostracized wife coming along beautifully. The preparation is charming, in the best boulevard manner. But when the situation arrives and has to be dealt with—what a mess, what falseness, what wrenching, what sickly smoothing, what ranting, and what terrific tediousness! It is so easy to begin. It is so easy to think of a fine idea. The next man you meet in a hotel bar will tell you a fine idea after two whiskeys—I mean a really fine idea. Only in art an idea doesn't exist till it is worked *out*. Brieux never (with the possible exception above mentioned) works an idea *out*. Because he can't. He doesn't know enough of his business. He can only do the easy parts of his business. Last autumn also, the Comédie Française revived "La Robe Rouge." The casting, owing to an effort to make it too good, was very bad; and the production was very bad, though Brieux himself superintended it. But, all allowances made for the inevitable turpitudes of this ridiculous national theatre, the play was senile; it was done for! Certainly it exposes the abuses of the French magistrature, but at what cost of fundamental truth! The melodramatic close might have been written in the Isle of Man. *17 Feb. '10*

Take the most notorious of all his plays, "Les Avariés." It contains an admirable sermon, a really effective sermon, animated by ideas which I suppose have been in the minds of exceptionally intelligent men for a hundred years or so, and which Brieux restated in terms of dramatic eloquence. But the sentimentality of the end is simply base. The sentimentality of another famous play, "Maternité," is even more deplorable.

It is said that Brieux's plays make you think. Well, it depends who you are. No, I will admit that they have several times made me think. I will admit that, since I saw "Les Avariés," I have never thought quite the same about syphilis as I did before. But what I say is that this has nothing to do with Brieux's position as a dramatist. Brieux could have written a pamphlet on the subject of "Les Avariés" which would have impressed me just as much

17 Feb. '10 as his play (I happened to read the play before I witnessed it). Indeed, if he had confined himself to a pamphlet I should have respected him more than I do. Brieux has never sharpened my sense of beauty; he has never made me see beauty where I had failed to see it. And this is what he ought to have done, as a serious dramatist. He is deficient in a feeling for beauty; he is deficient in emotion. But that is not the worst of him. Mr. Shaw is deficient in these supreme qualities. But Mr. Shaw is an honest playwright. And Brieux (speaking, of course, in a sense strictly artistic) is not. That he is dishonest in the cause of moral progress does not mitigate his crime. Zealots may deny this as loudly as they please. Nothing can keep Brieux's plays alive; they are bound to go precisely where the plays of Dumas *fils* have gone, because they are false to life. I do not expect to kill the oncoming craze, but I will give it no quarter.

C. E. MONTAGUE

I HAVE read Mr. C. E. Montague's "A Hind Let Loose" (Methuen, 6s.), and I am not going to advise anyone to follow my example. I do not desire to prejudice his circulation, but I have my conscience to consider. This is not a book for the intelligent masses; it would be folly to recommend it to them. It is for the secretly-arrogant few, those who really do "know that they are august" within, whatever garment of diffident and wild modesty they may offer to the world. Only those few can understand it. All admiration other than theirs will be either ignorant or dog-like—or both. Everybody on the Press will say that "A Hind Let Loose" is a novel about journalism. It is not. Journalism is merely the cloak hanging windily about it, as her cloak hung about Mrs. Colum Fay. It is a novel about the pride of the Ego. It is the fearful and yet haughty cry of originality against the vast tendency of the age, which tendency is that people should live in the age as in an intellectual barracks. Hedlum, the conversational clubman and successful barrister, is the real villain of the story, though he appears but for a moment. *10 Mar. '10*

10 Mar. '10 "Hedlum would take up all that was current, trim it and pare its nails, and give it his blessing and send it out into the world to get on, and it did famously. You felt that if it was not true then the fault was truth's; there must be some upper order of truth, not universally known, to which he had conformed and to which the facts, in the vulgar sense, could not have been loyal. All of him helped the effect. He was of the settled age—fifty or so—handsome, with the controlled benignity, the mellowed precision, the happy, distinguished melancholy sometimes united in a good-looking judge. . . . You watched the weighing of each word at its exit from the shaved, working lips, and the closure of their inexorable adamant behind its heels. As the last commonplace of club gossip, smoke-room heroics, and music-hall sentiment issued from these portals, transfigured by the moderate discount that made it twice itself, you not only saw it was final truth, or virility's quintessential emotion; you felt he had done something decisive, even gallant, and that you were in it—a fine fellow, too, in your way; and you quickened; you lived back and forward, back to the blithe days at school when they first taught you never to think your own thoughts or take what came in a way of your own, but to pool your brains with the rest and 'throw yourself into the life of the school,' and on to your early manhood's deeper training in resemblance to others, and so to the good day, always coming and always here, always to be had by him who wills it with his might, when the imitative shall inherit the earth." *10 Mar. '10*

I quote this, the very essence of the work, in order to choke off the feeble, the kind, and the altruistic. I would not hawk this book. If I had foreknown what it was I would never have mentioned it. I would have mentioned it to none, sure that, by the strange force of gravity which inevitably draws together a book and its fit reader, the novel would in the end reach the only audience worthy of it. I say no more about it.

PUBLISHERS AND AUTHORS

10 Mar. '10 AUTHENTIC documents are always precious to the student, and here is one which strikes me as precious beyond the ordinary. It is a letter received from a well-known publisher by a correspondent of mine who is a journalist:

"I am awfully sorry that we cannot take your novel, which is immensely clever, and which interested my partner more than anything he has read in a good while. He agrees with me, however, that it has not got the qualities that make for a sale, and you know that this is the great desideratum with the publisher. Now don't get peevish, and send us nothing else. I know you have a lot of talent, and your difficulty is in applying this talent to really practical problems rather than to the more attractive products of the imagination. Get down to facts, my son, and study your market. Find out what the people like to read and then write a story along those lines. This will bring you success, for you have a talent for success. Above all things, don't follow the lead of our headstrong friend who insists upon doing exactly what you have done in this novel, namely, neglecting the practical market and working out the fanciful dictates of imagination. Remember that novel-writing is as much of a business as making calico. If you write the novels that people want, you are going to sell them in bales. When you have made your name and your market, *then* you can afford to let your imagination run riot, and *then* people will look at you admiringly, and say, 'I don't understand this genius at all, but isn't he great?' Do you see the point? You must do this AFTER you have won your market, not before, and you can only win your market in the first place by writing what folks want to buy. — Sincerely yours——" *10 Mar. '10*

The writer is American. But the attitude of the average pushing English publisher could not have been more accurately expressed than in this letter sent by one New Yorker to another. The only thing that puzzles me is why the man originally chose books instead of calico. He would have sold more bales and made more money in calico. He would have understood calico better. In my opinion many publishers would have understood calico better than

10 Mar. '10 books. There are two things which a publisher ought to know about novel-producers—things which do not, curiously enough, apply to calico-producers, and which few publishers have ever grasped. I have known publishers go into the bankruptcy court and come out again safely and yet never grasp the significance of those two things. The first is that it is intensely stupid to ask a novelist to study the market with a view to obtaining large circulations. If he does not write to please himself—if his own taste does not naturally coincide with the taste of the million—he will never reach the million by taking thought. The Hall Caines, the Miss Corellis, and the Mrs. Humphry Wards are born, not made. It may seem odd, even to a publisher, that they write as they do write—by sheer glad instinct. But it is so. The second thing is that when a novelist has made "his name and his market" by doing one kind of thing he can't successfully go off at a tangent and do another kind of thing. To make the largest possible amount of money out of an artist the only way is to leave him alone. When will publishers grasp this? To make the largest possible amount of money out of an imitative hack, the only way is to leave him alone. When will publishers grasp that an imitative hack knows by the grace of God forty times more about the public taste than a publisher knows? *10 Mar. '10*

TOURGENIEFF AND DOSTOIEVSKY

31 Mar. '10 I HAVE read with very great interest Mr. Maurice Baring's new volume about Russia, "Landmarks in Russian Literature" (Methuen, 6s. net). It deals with Gogol, Tourgenieff, Dostoievsky, Tolstoy, and Tchehkoff. It is unpretentious. It is not "literary." I wish it had been more literary. Mr. Baring seems to have a greater love for literature than an understanding knowledge of it. He writes like a whole-hearted amateur, guided by commonsense and enthusiasm, but not by the delicate perceptions of an artist. He often says things, or says things in a manner, which will assuredly annoy the artist. Thus his curt, conventional remarks about Zola might have been composed for a leading article in the *Morning Post,* instead of for a volume of literary criticism. Nevertheless, I cannot be cross with him. In some ways his book is illuminating. I mean that it has illuminated my darkness. His chapters on Russian characteristics and on realism in Russian literature are genuinely valuable. In particular he makes me see that even French realism is an artificial and feeble growth compared with the spontaneous, unconscious realism of the Russians. If you talked to Russians about realism they probably would not know quite what you meant. And when you had at length made them understand they would certainly exclaim: "Well, of course! But why all this fuss about a simple matter?" Only a man who knows Russia very well, and who has a genuine affection for the Russian character, could have written these chapters. And I am ready to admit that they are more useful than many miles of appreciation in the delicate balancing manner of say an Arthur Symons. *31 Mar. '10*

Mr. Baring raises again the vexed question of Tourgenieff's position. It is notorious that Tourgenieff is much more highly appreciated outside Russia than in it. One is, of course, tempted to say that Russians cannot judge their own authors, for there is a powerful and morally overwhelming cult for Tourgenieff in France, Germany and England. I have myself said, sworn, and believed that "On the Eve" is the most perfect example of the novel yet produced in any country. And I am not sure that I am yet prepared to go back on

31 Mar. '10 myself. However, it is absurd to argue that Russians cannot judge their own authors. The best judges of Russian authors must be Russians. Think of the ridiculous misconceptions about English literature by first-class foreign critics! . . . But I am convinced that Mr. Baring goes too far in his statement of the Russian estimate of Tourgenieff. He says that educated Russian opinion would no more think of comparing Tourgenieff with Dostoievsky than educated English opinion would think of comparing Charlotte Yonge with Charlotte Brontë. This is absurd. Whatever may be Tourgenieff's general inferiority (and I do not admit it), he was a great artist and a complete artist. And he was a realist. There is all earth and heaven between the two Charlottes. One was an artist, the other was an excellent Christian body who produced stories that have far less relation to life than Frith's "Derby Day" has to the actual fact and poetry of Epsom. If Mr. Baring had bracketed Tourgenieff with Charlotte Brontë and Dostoievsky with the lonely Emily, I should have credited him with a subtle originality.

About half of the book is given to a straightforward, detailed, homely account of Dostoievsky, his character, genius, and works. It was very much wanted in English. I thought I had read all the chief works of the five great Russian novelists, but last year I came across one of Dostoievsky's, " The Brothers Karamazoff," of which I had not heard. It was a French translation, in two thick volumes. I thought it contained some of the greatest scenes that I had ever encountered in fiction, and I at once classed it with Stendhal's " Chartreuse de Parme " and Dostoievsky's " Crime and Punishment " as one of the supreme marvels of the world. Nevertheless, certain aspects of it puzzled me. When I mentioned it to friends I was told that I had gone daft about it, and that it was not a major work. Happening to meet Mrs. Garnett, the never-to-be-sufficiently-thanked translator of Tourgenieff and of Tolstoy, I made inquiries from her about it, and she said: " It is his masterpiece." We were then separated by a ruthless host, with my difficulties unsolved. I now learn from Mr. Baring that the French translation is bad and incomplete, and that the original work, vast as it is, is only a preliminary fragment of a truly *31 Mar. '10*

31 Mar. '10 enormous novel which death prevented Dostoievsky from finishing. Death, this is yet another proof of your astonishing clumsiness! The scene with the old monk at the beginning of "The Brothers Karamazoff" is in the very grandest heroical manner. There is nothing in either English or French prose literature to hold a candle to it. And really I do not exaggerate! There is probably nothing in Russian literature to match it, outside Dostoievsky. It ranks, in my mind, with the scene towards the beginning of "Crime and Punishment," when in the inn the drunken father relates his daughter's "shame." These pages are unique. They reach the highest and most terrible pathos that the novelist's art has ever reached. And if an author's reputation among people of taste depended solely on his success with single scenes Dostoievsky would outrank all other novelists, if not all poets. But it does not. Dostoievsky's works—all of them—have grave faults. They have especially the grave fault of imperfection, that fault which Tourgenieff and Flaubert avoided. They are tremendously unlevel, badly constructed both in large outline and in detail. The fact is that the difficulties under which he worked were too much for the artist in him. Mr. Baring admits these faults, but he does not sufficiently dwell on them. He glances at them and leaves them, with the result that the final impression given by his essay is apt to be a false one. Nobody, perhaps, ever understood and sympathized with human nature as Dostoievsky did. Indubitably nobody ever with the help of God and good luck ever swooped so high into tragic grandeur. But the man had fearful falls. He could not trust his wings. He is an adorable, a magnificent, and a profoundly sad figure in letters. He is anything you like. But he could not compass the calm and exquisite soft beauty of "On the Eve" or "A House of Gentlefolk." . . . *31 Mar. '10*

JOHN GALSWORTHY

14 July '10 MR. JOHN GALSWORTHY, whose volume of sketches, "A Motley," is now in process of being reviewed, is just finishing another novel, which will no doubt be published in the autumn. That novels have to be finished is the great disadvantage of the novelist's career—otherwise, as everyone knows, a bed of roses, a velvet cushion, a hammock under a ripe pear tree. To begin a novel is delightful. To finish it is the devil. Not because, on parting with his characters, the novelist's heart is torn by the grief which Thackeray described so characteristically. (The novelist who has put his back into a novel will be ready to kick the whole crowd of his characters down the front-door steps.) But because the strain of keeping a long book at the proper emotional level through page after page and chapter after chapter is simply appalling, and as the end approaches becomes almost intolerable. I have just finished a novel myself; my nineteenth, I think. So I know the rudiments of the experience. For those in peril on the sea, and for novelists finishing novels, prayers ought to be offered up.

JOHN GALSWORTHY

In accordance with my habit of re-reading books which have uncommonly interested me on first perusal, I have recently read again "A Man of Property." Well, it stands the test. It is certainly the most perfect of Mr. Galsworthy's novels up to now. Except for the confused impression caused by the too rapid presentation of all the numerous members of the Forsyte family at the opening, it has practically no faults. In construction it is unlike any other novel that I know, but that is not to say it has no constructive design—as some critics have said. It is merely to say that it is original. There are no weak parts in the book, no places where the author has stopped to take his breath and wipe his brow. The tension is never relaxed. This is one of the two qualities without which a novel cannot be first-class and great. The other is the quality of sound, harmonious design. Both qualities are exceedingly rare, and I do not know which is the rarer. In the actual material of the book, the finest quality is its extraordinary passionate cruelty towards the oppressors as distinguished from the oppressed. That oppressors should be treated with less sympathy than oppressed is contrary to my own notion of the ethics of *14 July '10*

14 July '10 creative art, but the result in Mr. Galsworthy's work is something very pleasing. Since "A Man of Property," the idea that the creator of the universe, or the Original Will, or whatever you like to call it or him, made a grotesque fundamental mistake in the conception of our particular planet has apparently gained much ground in Mr. Galsworthy's mind. I hope that this ground may slowly be recovered by the opposite idea. Anyhow, the Forsyte is universal. We are all Forsytes, just as we are all Willoughby Patternes, and this incontrovertible statement implies inevitably that Mr. Galsworthy is a writer of the highest rank. I re-read "The Man of Property" immediately after re-reading Dostoievsky's "Crime and Punishment," and immediately before re-reading Björnson's "Arne." It ranks well with these European masterpieces.

SUPPRESSIONS IN "DE PROFUNDIS"

21 July '10

SOME time ago I pointed out (what was to me a new discovery) that certain passages in the German translation of Oscar Wilde's "De Profundis" did not exist in the original English version as printed; and I suggested that Mr. Robert Ross, Oscar Wilde's faithful literary executor, should explain. He has been good enough to do so. He informs me that the passages in question were restored in the edition of "De Profundis" (the thirteenth) in Wilde's Complete Works, issued by Messrs. Methuen to a limited public, and that they have been retained in the fourteenth (separate) edition, of which Mr. Ross sends me a copy. I possessed only the first edition. I do not want to part with it, but the fourteenth is a great deal more interesting than the first. It contains a dedicatory letter by Mr. Ross to Dr. Max Meyerfeld ("But for you I do not think the book would ever have been published"), and some highly interesting letters written in Reading Gaol by Wilde to Mr. Ross (which had previously been published in Germany). In the course of this dedicatory letter, Mr. Ross says: "In sending copy

21 July '10 to Messrs. Methuen (to whom alone I submitted it) I anticipated refusal, as though the work were my own. A very distinguished man of letters who acted as their reader advised, however, its acceptance, and urged, in view of the uncertainty of its reception, the excision of certain passages, to which I readily assented."

This explains clearly enough the motive for suppressing the passages. But even after making allowance for the natural timidity and apprehensiveness of the publisher's reader, I cannot quite understand why those particular passages were cut out. Here is one of them: "I had genius, a distinguished name, high social position, brilliancy, intellectual daring; I made art a philosophy and philosophy an art. I altered the minds of men and the colours of things; there was nothing I said or did that did not make people wonder. I took the drama, the most objective form known to art, and made it as personal a mode of expression as the lyric or sonnet; at the same time I widened its range and enriched its characteristics. Drama, novel, poem in prose, poem in rhyme, subtle or fantastic dialogue, whatever I touched I made beautiful in a new mode of beauty. To truth itself I gave what is false no less than what is true as its rightful province, and showed that the false and the true are merely forms of intellectual existence. I treated art as the supreme reality and life as a mere mode of fiction. I awoke the imagination of my century so that it created myth and legend around me. I summed up all systems in a phrase, and all existence in an epigram. Along with these things I had things that were different. But I let myself be lured into long spells of senseless and sensual ease." It is difficult to see anything in the factitious but delightful brilliance of this very characteristic swagger that could have endangered the book's reception. *21 July '10*

Mr. Ross's letter to me concludes thus: "'De Profundis,' however, even in its present form, is only a fragment. The whole work could not be published in the lifetime of the present generation." This makes, within a month, the third toothsome dish as to which I have had the exasperating news that it is being reserved for that spoiled child, posterity. I may say, however, that I do not regard "De Profundis" as one of Wilde's best books. I was disappointed

21 July '10 with it. It is too frequently insincere, and the occasion was not one for pose. And it has another fault. I happened to meet M. Henry Davray several times while he was translating the book into French. M. Davray's knowledge of English is profound, and I was accordingly somewhat disconcerted when one day, pointing to a sentence in the original, he asked, "What does that mean?" I thought, "Is Davray at last 'stumped'?" I examined the sentence with care, and then answered, "It doesn't mean anything." "I thought so," said M. Davray. We looked at each other. M. Davray was an old friend of Wilde's, and was one of the dozen men who attended his desolating funeral. And I was an enthusiastic admirer of Wilde's style at its best. We said no more. But a day or two later a similar incident happened, and yet another.

Wilde's letters to Mr. Ross from prison are extremely good. They begin sombrely, but after a time the wit lightens, and towards the end it is playing continually. The first gleam of it is this: "I am going to take up the study of German. Indeed prison seems to be the proper place for such a study." On the subject of the natural life, he says a thing which is exquisitely wise: "Stevenson's letters are most disappointing also. I see that romantic surroundings are the worst surroundings for a romantic writer. In Gower Street Stevenson would have written a new 'Trois Mousquetaires,' in Samoa he writes letters to the *Times* about Germans. I see also the traces of a terrible strain to lead a natural life. To chop wood with any advantage to oneself or profit to others, one should not be able to describe the process. In point of fact the natural life is the unconscious life. Stevenson merely extended the sphere of the artificial by taking to digging. The whole dreary book has given me a lesson. If I spend my future life reading Baudelaire in a café I shall be leading a more natural life than if I take to hedger's work or plant cacao in mud-swamps." *21 July '10*

HOLIDAY READING

4 Aug '10 I CAME away for a holiday without any books, except one, and I cut off the whole of my supply of newspapers, except one. As a rule my baggage is most injurious to railway porters, and on the Continent very costly, because of the number of books and neckties it contains. I wear the neckties, but I never read the books. I am always meaning to read them, but something is always preventing me. Before starting, the awful thought harasses me: Supposing I wanted to read and I had naught! This time I decided that it would be agreeably perilous to run the risk. The unique book which I packed was the sixth volume of Montaigne in the Temple Classics edition. We are all aware, from the writings of Mr. A. B. Walkley, Sir William Robertson Nicoll, Mr. Hall Caine and others, what a peerless companion is Montaigne; how in Montaigne there is a page to suit every mood; how the most diverse mentalities—the pious, the refined, the libertine, the philosophic, the egoistic, the altruistic, the merely silly—may find in him the food of sympathy. I knew I should be all right with Montaigne. I invariably read in bed of a night (unless paying in my temples the price of excess), and nobody who ever talked about bed-books has succeeded in leaving out Montaigne from his list. My luggage cost much less than usual. I positively looked forward to reading Montaigne. Yet when the first night in a little French hotel arrived, and I had perched the candle on the top of the ewer on the night-table in order to get it high enough, I discovered that instead of Montaigne I was going to read a verbatim account of a poisoning trial in the Paris *Journal*. That is about three weeks ago, and I have not yet opened my Montaigne, I have, however, talked enthusiastically to sundry French people about Montaigne, and explained to them that Florio's translation is at least equal to the original, and that Montaigne is truly beloved and understood in England alone. *4 Aug '10*

It was on the second day of my holiday, in another small provincial town in central France, where I was improving my mind and fitting myself for cultured society in London by the contemplation of cathedrals, that I came across, in a draper's and fancy-ware shop a remaindered stock of French fiction, at 4½d. the volume. Among these, to my

4 Aug '10 intense disgust, was a translation of a little thing of my own, and also a collection of stories by Léonide Andreief, translated by Serger Persky, and published by *Le Monde Illustré*. Although I already possessed, in Montaigne, sustenance for months, I bought this volume, and at once read it. A small book by Andreief, "The Seven that were Hanged," was published in England—last year, I think—by Mr. Fifield. It received a very great deal of praise, and was, in fact, treated as a psychological masterpiece. I was disappointed with it myself, for the very simple reason that I found it tedious. I had difficulty in finishing it. I gather that Andreief has a great reputation in Russia, sharing with Gorky the leadership of the younger school. Well, I don't suppose that I shall ever read any more Gorky, who has assuredly not come up to expectations. There are things among the short stories of Andreief (the volume is entitled "Nouvelles") which are better than "The Seven that were Hanged." "The Governor," for example, is a pretty good tale, obviously written under the influence of Tolstoy's "Death of Ivan Ilyitch"; and a story about waiting at a railway station remains in the mind not unpleasantly. But the best of the book is second-rate, vitiated by diffuseness, imitativeness and the usual sentimentality. Neither Andreief nor Gorki will ever seriously count. Neither of them comes within ten leagues of the late Anton Tchehkoff. I think there must be young novelists alive in Russia who are superior to these two alleged leaders. I have, in fact, heard talk of one Apouktine, in this country of France, and I am taking measures to read him. *4 Aug '10*

When at length I settled down in a small hotel in a village on the further coast of Brittany, I had read nothing but Andreief and criminal processes. Nobody else in the hotel, save one old lady, read anything but criminal processes. It is true that it was a sadly vulgar hotel. My fellow-guests were mainly employees who had escaped for a fortnight from the big Paris shops. In particular there was a handsome young woman from the fur department of the Grands Magasins du Louvre, who (weather permitting) spent half her morning in a kimono at her bedroom window while her husband (perfumery department) discussed patriotism and feminism in the café below. When I remember the spectacle, which I

4 Aug '10 have often seen, of the staff of the Grands Magasins du Louvre trooping into its prison at 7.30 a.m. to spend a happy day of eleven and a half hours in humouring the whims of the great shopping classes, I was charmed to watch this handsome and vapid creature idling away whole hours at her window and enjoying the gaze of persons like myself. She never read. Once when I had a bit of a discussion with her husband at lunch upon an intellectual matter, she got up and walked away with an impatient gesture of disdain, as if to say: "What has all this got to do with Love?" Her husband never read, either. Their friends did not read, not even newspapers. But another couple had an infant, aged three, and this infant had a rather fierce grandmother, and this grandmother read a great deal. She and I alone stood for literature. She would stay at home with the infant while the intermediate generation was away larking. She was always reading the same book. It was a thick book, with a glossy coloured cover displaying some scene in which homicide and passion were mingled; its price, new, was sixpence halfpenny, and its title was simply and magnificently, "Borgia!" with a note of exclamation after it. She confined herself

to "Borgia!" She was tireless with "Borgia!" She went home to Paris reading "Borgia!" It was a shocking hotel, so different from the literary hotels of Switzerland, Bournemouth, and Scarborough, where all the guests read Meredith and Walter Pater. I ought to have been ashamed to be seen in such a place. My only excuse is that the other two hotels in the remote little village were just as bad, probably worse. *4 Aug '10*

THE BRITISH ACADEMY OF LETTERS

18 Aug. '10 A CORRESPONDENT writes angrily to me because I have not written angrily about the list of authors recently put forward as Academicians of the proposed new British Academy of Letters. The fact is that the entire scheme of the British Academy of Letters had a near shave of escaping my attention altogether. I only heard of it by accident, being away on a holiday in a land where they have had enough of academies. But for the miracle of a newspaper found on a fishing boat I might not have even known what on earth my correspondent was raging about. In literary circles such as mine the new British Academy of Letters has not been extensively advertised. In the main I agree with my correspondent's criticisms of the list. But I must say that his ire shows a certain naïveté. None but a young and trustful man could have expected the list to be otherwise than profoundly and utterly grotesque. A list of creative artists that did not suffer acutely from this defect could only be compiled by creative artists themselves. Not all, and not nearly all, creative artists would be qualified to sit on the compiling committee, but nobody who was not a creative artist would be qualified. The rest of the world has no sure ground of judgment, for the true critical faculty is inseparable from the creative. The least critical word of the most prejudiced and ignorant creative artist is more valuable than whole volumes writ by dilettanti of measureless refinement and erudition. I am not aware of the identity of the persons who sat down together and compiled the pleasing preliminary list of twenty-seven academicians, but I am perfectly certain that the predominant among them were not original artists. The artist, at the present stage of social evolution, would as soon think of worrying himself about the formation of an academy, as of putting up for the St. Pancras Borough Council. He has something else to do. He fears the deadly contacts with those prim, restless, and tedious dilettanti. And of course he knows that academies are the enemies of originality and progress. *18 Aug. '10*

That list was undoubtedly sketched out by a coterie of dilettanti. London swarms with the dilettanti of letters. They do not belong to the criminal classes, but their good

18 Aug. '10 intentions, their culture, their judiciousness, and their infernal cheek amount perhaps to worse than arson or assault. Their attitude towards the creative artist is always one of large, tolerant pity. They honestly think that if only the artist knew his business as they know his business, if only he had their discernment and impartiality, and if only he wasn't so confoundedly ignorant and violent—how different he would be, how much nicer and better, how much more effective! They are eternally ready to show an artist where he is wrong and what he ought to do in order to obtain their laudations unreserved. In a personal encounter, they will invariably ride over him like a regiment of polite cavalry, because they are accustomed to personal encounters. They shine at tea, at dinner, and after dinner. They talk more easily than he does, and write more easily too. They can express themselves more readily. And they know such a deuce of a lot. And they can balance pros and cons with astonishing virtuosity. The Press is their washpot. And they are influential in other places. They can get pensions for their favourites. They know the latest methods of pulling an artichoke to pieces. And they will say among themselves, forgiving but slightly pained: "Yes, he's written a very remarkable novel, but he doesn't know how to eat an artichoke." They would be higher than the angels were it not for the fact that, in art, they are exquisitely and perfectly footling. They cannot believe this, the public cannot believe it. Nevertheless, every artist knows it to be true. They have never done anything themselves except fuss around. *18 Aug. '10*

As for us, we are their hobby. And since unoriginality is their most striking characteristic, some of us are occasionally pretty nearly hobbied to extinction by them. In every generation they select some artist, usually for reasons quite unconnected with art, and put him exceedingly high up in a niche by himself. And when you name his name you must hush your voice, and discussion ends. Thus in the present generation, in letters, they have selected Joseph Conrad, a great artist, but not the only artist on the island. When Conrad is mentioned they say, "Ah, Conrad!" and bow the head. And in the list, compiled presumably to represent what is finest in English literature at an epoch when the

18 Aug. '10 novel is admittedly paramount, there are half a dozen of everything except novelists. There is only one practising novelist, and he is not an Englishman. I said a moment ago that the most striking characteristic of the dilettanti is unoriginality. But possibly a serene unhumorousness runs it close.

The master-thought at the bottom of this scheme is not an Academy of British Letters for literary artists, but an Academy of British Letters for literary dilettanti. A few genuine artists, if the scheme blossoms, will undoubtedly be found in it. But that will be an accident. Some of the more decorative dilettanti have had a vision of themselves as academicians. Hence the proposal for an academy. In the public mind dillettanti are apt to be confused with artists. Indeed, the greater the artist, the more likely the excellent public is to regard him as a sort of inferior and unserious barbaric dilettante. (Fortunately posterity does not make these mistakes.) A genuine original artist is bound to make a sad spectacle of himself in an academy. Knowing this, Anatole France, the greatest man in the Académie Française, never goes near the sittings. He has got from the institution all that advantage of advertisement which he was legitimately entitled to get, and he has no further use for the Académie Française. His contempt for it as an artist is not concealed. What can academicians do except put on a uniform and make eulogistic discourses to each other under the eyes of fashionably-attired American female tourists? The Authors' Society does more practical good for the art of literature in a year than an Academy of Letters could do in forty years. *18 Aug. '10*

The existing British Academy of Learning may or may not be a dignified and serious institution. I do not know. But I see no reason why it should not be. It has not interested the public, and it never will. Advertisement does not enter into it to any appreciable extent. Moreover, it is much more difficult to be a dilettante of learning than a dilettante of letters. You are sooner found out. Further, learning can be organized, and organized with advantage. Creative art cannot. All artistic academies are bad. The one real use of an artistic academy is to advertise the art which it represents, to cause the excellent public to think and chatter about that art and to support it by

18 Aug. '10 buying specimens of it. The Royal Academy has admirably succeeded in this business, as may be seen at Burlington Gardens any afternoon in the season. But it has succeeded at the price of making itself grotesque and vicious; and it retards, though of course it cannot stop, the progress of graphic art. Certain arts are in need of advertisement. For example, sculpture. An Academy of Sculpture might, just now, do some good and little harm. But literature is in no need of advertisement in this country. It is advertised more than all the others arts put together. It includes the theatre. It is advertised to death. Be sure that if it really did stand in need of advertisement, no dilettante would have twice looked at it. The one point which interests me about the proposed academy is whether uniforms are comprised in the scheme.

UNFINISHED PERUSALS

ONE of the moral advantages of not being a regular professional, labelled, literary critic is that when one has been unable to read a book to the end, one may admit the same cheerfully. It often happens to the professional critic not to be able to finish a book, but of course he must hide the weakness, for it is his business to get to the end of books whether they weary him or not. It is as much his living to finish reading a book as it is mine to finish writing a book. Twice lately I have got ignominiously "stuck" in novels, and in each case I particularly regretted the sad breakdown. Gabriele d'Annunzio's "Forse che si forse che no" has been my undoing. I began it in the French version by Donatella Cross (Calmann-Lévy, 3 frs. 50c.), and I began it with joy and hope. The translation, by the way, is very good. Whatever mountebank tricks d'Annunzio may play as a human being, he has undoubtedly written some very great works. He is an intensely original artist. You may sometimes think him silly, foppish, extravagant, or even caddish (as in "Il Fuoco"), but you have to admit that the English notions of what *25 Aug. '10*

25 Aug. '10 constitutes extravagance or caddishness are by no means universally held. And anyhow you have to admit that there is a man who really holds an attitude towards life, who is steeped in the sense of style, and who has a superb passion for beauty. Some of d'Annunzio's novels were a revelation, dazzling. And who that began even "Il Fuoco" could resist it? How adult, how subtle, how (in the proper signification) refined, seems the sexuality of d'Annunzio after the timid, gawky, infantile, barbaric sexuality of our "island story"! People are not far wrong on the Continent when they say, as they do say, that English novelists cannot deal with an Englishwoman—or could not up till a few years ago. They never get into the same room with her. They peep like schoolboys through the crack of the door. D'Annunzio can deal with an Italian woman. He does so in the first part of "Forse che si forse che no." She is only one sort of woman, but she *is* one sort—and that's something! He has not done many things better than the long scene in the Mantuan palace. There is nothing to modern British taste positively immoral in this first part, but it is tremendously sexual. It contains a description of a kiss—just a kiss and nothing more—that is magnificent and overwhelming. You may say that you don't want a magnificent and overwhelming description of a kiss in your fiction. To that I reply that I do want it. Unfortunately d'Annunzio leaves the old palace and goes out on to the aviation ground, and, for me, gradually becomes unreadable. The agonies that I suffered night after night fighting against the wild tedium of d'Annunzio's airmanship, and determined that I would find out what he was after or perish, and in the end perishing—in sleep! To this hour I don't know for sure what he was driving at—what is the theme of the book! But if his theme is what I dimly guess it to be, then the less said about it the better in Britain. *25 Aug. '10*

The other book which has engaged me in a stand-up fight and floored me is A. F. Wedgwood's "The Shadow of a Titan" (Duckworth, 6s.). For this I am genuinely sorry; I had great hopes of it. I was seriously informed that "The Shadow of a Titan" is a first-class thing, something to make one quote Keats "On First Reading Chapman's 'Homer.'" A most extraordinary review of it appeared in the *Manchester*

25 Aug. '10 *Guardian,* a newspaper not given to facile enthusiasms about new writers, and a paper which, on the whole, reviews fiction more capably and conscientiously than any other daily in the kingdom. Well, I wouldn't care to say anything more strongly in favour of "The Shadow of a Titan" than that it is clever. Clever it is, especially in its style. The style has the vulgarly glittering cleverness of, say, Professor Walter Raleigh. It is exhausting, and not a bit beautiful. The author—whoever he may be; the name is quite unfamiliar to me, but this is not the first time he has held a pen—chooses his material without originality. Much of it is the common material of the library novel, seen and handled in the common way. When I was floored I had just got to a part which disclosed the epical influence of Mr. Joseph Conrad. It had all the characteristics of Mr. Conrad save his deep sense of form and his creative genius. . . . . However, I couldn't proceed with it. In brief, for me, it was dull. Probably the latter half was much better, but I couldn't cut my way through to the latter half.

MR. A. C. BENSON

I AM indebted to Mr. Murray for sending what is to me a new manifestation of the entirely precious activity of Mr. Arthur Christopher Benson. Mr. Benson, in "The Thread of Gold," ministers to all that is highest and most sacred in the Mudie temperament. It is not a new book; only I have been getting behindhand. It was first printed in 1905, and it seems to have been on and off the printing-presses ever since, and now Mr. Murray has issued it, very neatly, at a shilling net, so that people who have never even been inside Mudie's may obtain it. I have read the book with intense joy, hugging myself, and every now and then running off to a sister-spirit with a "I say, just listen to *this*!" The opening sentence of one of the various introductions serves well to display Mr. A. C. Benson at his superlative: "I have for a great part of my life desired, perhaps more than I have desired anything else, to make a beautiful book; and I have tried, perhaps too hard and too often, to do this, *without ever quite succeeding*" [my italics]. Oh, triple modesty! The violet-like beauty of that word "quite"! Thus he tried perhaps *1 Sep. '10*

1 Sep. '10 too hard and too often to produce something beautiful! Not that for a moment I believe the excellent Mr. Benson to be so fatuous as these phrases, like scores of others in the book, would indicate. It is merely that heaven has been pleased to deprive him of any glimmer of humour, and that he is the victim of a style which, under an appearance of neatness and efficiency and honesty, is really disorderly, loose, inefficient and traitorous. His pages abound in instances of the unfaithfulness of his style, which is continually giving him away and making him say what he does not in fact want to say. For example: "Such traces as one sees in the chapels of the Oxford Movement. . . . Would be purely deplorable from the artistic point of view, if they did not possess a historical interest." As if historical interest could make them less deplorable from an artistic point of view! It might make them less deplorable from another point of view. Three times he explains the motif of the book. Here is the third and, at present, the last version of the motif: "That whether we are conquerors or conquered, triumphant or despairing, prosperous or pitiful, well or ailing, we are all these things through Him that loves us." I seem to remember that the late Frances Ridley *1 Sep. '10* Havergal burst into the world with this information. I recommend her works to Mr. Benson. In another of the introductions he says: "I think that God put it into my heart to write this book, and I hope that he [not He] will allow me to persevere." Personally (conceited though I am), I never put myself to the trouble of formulating hopes concerning the Infinite Purpose, but if I did I should hope that He just won't. Mr. Benson proceeds: "And yet indeed I know that I am not fit for so holy a task." Here we have one of the most diverting instances of Mr. Benson's trick-playing style. He didn't mean that; he only said it. Much, if not most, of "The Thread of of Gold" is merely absurd. Some of it is pretentious, some of it inept. All of it is utterly banal. All of it has the astounding calm assurance of mediocrity. It is a solemn thought that tens of thousands of well-dressed mortals alive and idle to-day consider themselves to have been uplifted by the perusal of this work. It is also a solemn thought that God in His infinite mercy and wisdom is still allowing Mr. Benson to persevere in his so holy a task, thus responding to Mr. Benson's hopes.

THE LITERARY PERIODICAL

8 Sep. '10 I HAVE just had news of a purely literary paper which is shortly to be started. I do not mean a paper devoted to literary criticisms chiefly, but chiefly to creative work. This will be something of a novelty in England. Its founders are two men who possess, happily, a practical acquaintance with publishing. The aim of the paper will be to print, and to sell, imaginative writing of the highest character. Its purpose is artistic, and neither political nor moral. Dangers and difficulties lie before an enterprize of this kind. The first and the principal difficulty will be the difficulty of obtaining the high-class stuff in sufficient quantities to fill the paper. The rate of pay will not and cannot be high, and authors capable of producing really high-class stuff —I mean stuff high-class in execution as well as in intention—are strangely keen on getting the best possible remuneration for it. Idle to argue that genuine artists ought to be indifferent to money! They are not. And what is still more curious, they will seldom produce their best work unless they really do want money. This is a fact which will stand against all the sentimental denyings of dilettanti. And, of course, genuine artists are quite right in getting every cent they can. The richest of them don't get enough. But even if the rates of pay of the new organ were high, the difficulty would still be rather acute, because the whole mass of really high-class stuff produced is relatively very small. High-class stuff is like radium. And the number of men who can produce it is strictly limited. There are dozens and scores of men who can write stuff which has all the mannerisms and external characteristics of high-class stuff, but which is not high-class. Extinct exotic periodicals, such as the *Yellow Book,* the *Savoy,* the *Dial,* the *Anglo-Saxon,* and such publications as the *Neolith,* richly prove this. What was and is the matter with all of them is literary priggishness, and dullness. One used to read them more often as a duty than as a pleasure. *8 Sep. '10*

A great danger is the inevitable tendency to disdain the public, and to appeal only to artists. Artists, like washerwomen, cannot live on one another. Moreover, nobody has any right to disdain the public. You will find that, as a general rule, the greatest artists have managed to get and to keep

8 Sep. '10 on good terms with the public. If an artist is clever enough—if he is not narrow, insolent, and unbalanced—he will usually contrive while pleasing himself to please the public, or *a* public. It is his business to do so. If he does not do so he proves himself incompetent. He is merely mumbling to himself. Just as the finite connotes the infinite, so an artist connotes a public. The artist who says he doesn't care a fig for the public is a liar. He may have many admirable virtues, but he is a liar. The tragedy of all the smaller literary periodicals in France is that the breach between them and the public is complete. They are unhealthy, because they have not sufficient force to keep themselves alive, and they make no effort to acquire that force. They scorn that force. They are kept alive by private subsidies. A paper cannot be established in a fortnight, but no artistic paper which has no reasonable prospect of paying its way ought to continue to exist; for it demonstrates nothing but an obstinacy which is ridiculous. The first business of the editor of an artistic periodical is to interest the public in questions of art. He cannot possibly convince them till he has interested them up to the point of regularly listening to him. Enthusiastic artists are apt to forget this. It is no use being brilliant and conscientious on a tub at a street corner unless you can attract some kind of a crowd. The public has just got to be considered. You may say that it is not easy to make any public listen to the truth about anything. Well, of course, it isn't. But it can be done by tact, and tact, and tact. *8 Sep. '10*

I do not think that there is a remunerative public in England for any really literary paper which entirely bars politics and morals. England is not an artistic country, in the sense that Latin countries are artistic, and no end can be served by pretending that it is. Its serious interests are political and moral. Personally, I fail to see how politics and morals can be separated from art. I should be very sorry to separate my art from my politics. And I am convinced that the conductors of the new organ will perceive later, if not sooner, that political and moral altercations must not be kept out of their columns. At any rate they will have to be propagandist, pugilistic, and even bloodthirsty. They will have to formulate a creed, and to try to ram it down people's

8 Sep. '10 throats. To print merely so many square feet of the best obtainable imaginative stuff and to let the stuff speak for itself will assuredly not suffice in this excellent country.

My mind returns to the exceeding difficulty of obtaining the right contributors. English editors have never appreciated the importance of this. As English manufacturers sit still and wait for customers, so English editors sit still and wait for contributors. The interestingness of the *New Age,* if I may make an observation which the editorial pen might hesitate to make, is due to the fact that contributors have always been searched for zealously and indefatigably. They have been compelled to come in—sometimes with a lasso, sometimes with a revolver, sometimes with a lure of flattery; but they have been captured. American editors are much better than English editors in this supreme matter. The profound truth has not escaped them that good copy does not as a rule fly in unbidden at the office window. They don't idiotically pretend that they have far more of the right kind of stuff than they know what to do with, as does the medium-fatuous English editor. They cajole. They run round. They hustle. The letters which

I get from American editors are one of the joys of my simple life. They are so un-English. They write: "Won't you be good enough to let us hear from you?" Or, "We are anxious [underlined] to see your output." Imagine that from an English editor! And they contrive to say what they mean, picturesquely. One editor wrote me: "We want material that will hit the mark without producing either insomnia or heart-failure." An editor capable of such self-expression endears himself at once to any possible contributor. And, above all, they do not fear each other, as ours do, nor tremble at the thought of Mrs. Grundy (I mean the best ones). A letter which I received only a few days ago ended thus: "We are not running the magazine for the benefit of the Young Person, and we are not afraid of Realism so long as it is interesting. Hoping to hear from you." I lay these paragraphs respectfully at the feet of the conductors of the new paper. *8 Sep. '10*

THE LENGTH OF NOVELS

22 Sep. '10 It happened lately to a lady who is one of the pillars of the *British Weekly* to state in her column of innocuous gossip about clothes, weather, and holidays, that a hundred thousand words or three hundred and fifty pages was the "comfortable limit" for a novel. I feel sure she meant no harm by it, and that she attached but little importance to it. The thing was expressed with a condescension which was perhaps scarcely becoming in a paragraphist, but such accidents will happen even in the most workmanlike columns of gossip, and are to be forgiven. Nevertheless, the *Westminster Gazette* has seized hold of the paragraph, framed it in 22-carat gold, and hung it up for observation, and a magnificent summer correspondence has blossomed round about it, to the great profit of the *Westminster Gazette* which receives, gratis, daily about a column and a half of matter signed by expensive names. Other papers, daily and weekly, have also joined in the din and the fray. As the discussion is perfectly futile, I do not propose to add to it. In spite of the more or less violent expression of preferences, nobody really cares whether a novel is long or short. In spite of the fact that a certain type of mind, common among publishers, is always apt to complain that novels at a given moment are either too long or too short, the length of a novel has no influence whatever on its success or failure. One of the most successful novels of the present generation, "Ships that Pass in the Night," is barely 60,000 words long. One of the most successful novels of the present generation, "The Heavenly Twins," is quite 200,000 words long. Both were of the right length for the public. As for the mid-Victorian novels, most of the correspondents appear to have a very vague idea of their length. It is said they "exceed 200,000 words." It would be within the mark to say that they exceed 400,000 words. There is not one of them, however, that would not be tremendously improved by being cut down to about half. And even then the best of them would not compare with "The Mayor of Casterbridge" or "Nostromo," or "The Way of all Flesh." The damning fault of all mid-Victorian novels is that they are incurably ugly and sentimental. Novelists had not yet discovered that the first business of a work of art is to be beautiful, and its second not to be sentimental. *22 Sep. 10*

ARTISTS AND MONEY

6 *Oct.* '10 A MONTH ago, à propos of the difficulties of running a high-class literary periodical, I wrote the following words: "Idle to argue that genuine artists ought to be indifferent to money! They are not. And what is still more curious, they will seldom produce their best work unless they really do want money." This pronouncement came at an unfortunate moment, which was the very moment when Mr. Sampson happened to be denying, with a certain fine heat, the thesis of Lord Rosebery that poverty is good for poets. Somebody even quoted me against Mr. Sampson in favour of Lord Rosebery. This I much regret, and it has been on my mind ever since. I do not wish to be impolite on the subject of Lord Rosebery. He is an ageing man, probably exacerbated by the consciousness of failure. At one time—many years ago—he had his hours of righteous enthusiasm. And he has always upheld the banner of letters in a social sphere whose notorious proud stupidity has been immemorially blind to the true function of art in life. But if any remark of Lord Rosebery's at a public banquet could fairly be adduced in real support of an argument

of mine, I should be disturbed. And, in fact, I heartily agreed with Mr. Sampson's demolishment of Lord Rosebery's speech about genius and poverty. Lord Rosebery was talking nonsense, and as with all his faults he cannot be charged with the stupidity of his class, he must have known that he was talking nonsense. The truth is that as the official mouthpiece of the nation he was merely trying to excuse, in an official perfunctory way, the inexcusable behaviour of the nation towards its artists. *6 Oct. '10*

As regards my own assertion that genuine artists will seldom produce their best work unless they really do want money, I fail to see how it conspires with Lord Rosebery's assertion. Moreover, I must explain that I was not thinking of poets. I was thinking of prose-writers, who do have a chance of making a bit of money. Money has scarcely any influence on the activity of poets, because they are aware that, no matter how well they succeed, the chances are a million to one against any appreciable monetary reward. An extreme lack of money will, of course, hamper them, and must, of course, do harm to the artist in them. An assured plenty of money may conceivably induce

6 Oct. '10 lethargy. But the hope of making money by their art will not spur them on, for there is no hope. No! I ought to have said explicitly at the time that I had in mind, not poets, who by the indifference of the public are set apart from money, but of those artists who have a reasonable opportunity of becoming public darlings and of earning now and then incomes which a grocer would not despise. That these latter are constantly influenced by money, and spurred to their finest efforts by the need of the money necessary for the satisfaction of their tastes, is a fact amply proved by the experience of everybody who is on intimate terms with them in real life. It almost amounts to common literary knowledge. It applies equally to the mediocre and to the distinguished artist. Those persons who have not participated in the pleasures and the pains of intimacy with distinguished writers depending for a livelihood on their pens can learn the truth about them by reading the correspondence of such authors as Scott, Balzac, Dickens, de Maupassant, and Stevenson. It is an absolute certainty that we owe about half the "Comédie Humaine" to Balzac's extravagant imprudence. It is equally sure that

Scott's mania for landed estate was responsible for a very considerable part of his artistic output. And so on. When once an artist has "tasted" the money of art, the desire thus set up will keep his genius hard at work better than any other incentive. It occasionally happens that an artist financially prudent, after doing a few fine things, either makes or comes into so much money that he is wealthy for the rest of his life. Such a condition induces idleness, induces a disinclination to fight against artistic difficulties. Naturally! I could give living instances in England to-day. But my discretion sends me to France for an instance. Take François de Curel. François de Curel was writing, twenty years ago, dramatic works of the very best kind. Their value was acknowledged by the few, and it remains permanent. The author is definitely classed as a genius in the history of the French theatre. But the verdict has not yet been endorsed by the public. For quite a number of years M. de Curel has produced practically nothing on the stage. He has preferred to withdraw from the battle against the indifference of the public. Had he needed money, the hope of money would have forced him to continue the battle, and *6 Oct. '10*

6 Oct. '10 we should have had perhaps half a dozen really fine plays by François de Curel that do not at present exist. But he did not need money. He is in receipt of a large income from iron foundries.

HENRI BECQUE

HENRI BECQUE, one of the greatest dramatists of the nineteenth century, and certainly the greatest realistic French dramatist, died at the close of the century in all the odour of obliquity. His work is now the chief literary topic in Paris; it has indeed rivalled the Portuguese revolution and the French railway strike as a subject of conversation among people who talk like sheep run. This dizzy popularity has been due to an accident, but it is, nevertheless, a triumph for Becque, who until recently had won the esteem only of the handful of people who think for themselves. I should say that no first-class modern French author is more perfectly unknown and uncared-for in England than Henri Becque. I once met a musical young woman who had never heard of Ibsen (she afterwards married a man with twelve thousand a year—such is life!), but I have met dozens and scores of enormously up-to-date persons who had never heard of Henri Becque. The most fantastic and the most exotic foreign plays have been performed in England, but I doubt if the London curtain has ever yet risen on a play of Becque's. Once in Soho, a historic and *20 Oct. '10*

20 Oct. '10 highly ceremonious repast took place. I entertained a personage to afternoon tea in a restaurant where afternoon tea had never been served before. This personage was the President of the Incorporated Stage Society. He asked me if I knew anything about a French play called "La Parisienne." I replied that I had seen it oftener than any other modern play, and that it was the greatest modern play of my acquaintance. He then enquired whether I would translate it for the Stage Society. I said I should be delighted to translate it for the Stage Society. He expressed joy and said the Committee would sit on the project. I never heard any more.

Becque wrote two absolutely first-class modern realistic plays. One is "La Parisienne." The other is "Les Corbeaux." Once, when I was in Paris, I saw exposed among a million other books in front of the window of Stock's shop near the Théâtre Français a copy of "Les Corbeaux." Opening it, I perceived that it was an example of the first edition (1882). I asked the price, and to my horror the attendant hesitated and said that he would "see." I feared the price was going to be fancy.

He came back and named four francs, adding, "It's our last copy." I paid the four francs willingly. On examining my trophy I saw that it was published by Tresse. Now Stock became Tresse's partner before he had that business to himself. I had simply bought the play at the original house of its publication. And it had fallen to me, after some twenty-five years, to put the first edition of "Les Corbeaux" out of print! I went home and read the play and was somewhat disappointed with it. I thought it very fine in its direct sincerity, but not on the same plane as "La Parisienne." *20 Oct. '10*

Antoine, founder of the Théâtre Libre, director of the Théâtre Antoine during brilliant years, and now director of the Odéon (which he has raised from the dead), was always a tremendous admirer of Becque. It was through Antoine that Paris had such magnificent performances of "La Parisienne." He had long expressed his intention of producing "Les Corbeaux," and now he has produced "Les Corbeaux" at the Odéon, where it has been definitely accepted and consecrated as a masterpiece. I could not refrain from going to Paris

20 Oct. '10 specially to see it. It was years since I had been in the Odéon. Rather brighter, perhaps, in its more ephemeral decorations, but still the same old-fashioned, roomy, cramped, provincial theatre, with pit-tier boxes like the cells of a prison! The audience was good. It was startlingly good for the Odéon. The play, too, at first seemed old-fashioned—in externals. It has bits of soliloquies and other dodges of technique now demoded. But the first act was not half over before the extreme modernness of the play forced itself upon you. Tchehkoff is not more modern. The picture of family life presented in the first act was simply delightful. All the bitterness was reserved for the other acts. And what superb bitterness! No one can be so cruel as Becque to a "sympathetic" character. He exposes every foolishness of the ruined widow; he never spares her for an instant; and yet one's sympathy is not alienated. This is truth. This is a play. I had not read the thing with sufficient imagination, with the result that for me it "acted" much better than it had "read." Its sheer beauty, truth, power, and wit justified even the great length of the last act. I though Becque had continued to add scenes to the play after it was essentially finished. But it was I who was mistaken, not he. The final scene began by irritating and ended by completely capturing the public. Teissier, the principal male part, was played by M. Numès in a manner which amounted to genius. *20 Oct. '10*

"Les Corbeaux" was originally produced at the Théâtre Français, where it was not a success. All Becque's recent fame is due, after Becque, to Antoine. But now that Antoine has done all the hard work, Jules Claretie, the flaccid director of the Français, shows a natural desire to share in the harvest. Becque left a play unfinished, "Les Polichinelles." Becque's executor, M. Robaglia, handed this play to M. Henri de Noussanne to finish—heaven knows why! M. de Noussanne has written novels entirely bereft of importance, and he is the editor of "Gil Blas," a daily paper whose importance it would not be easy to under-estimate; and his qualifications for finishing a play by Becque are in the highest degree mysterious. The finished play was to be produced at the Français. The production would have been what the French call a solemnity. But M. Robaglia suddenly jibbed. He declared

20 Oct. '10 M. de Noussanne's work to be unworthy, and he declined to permit the performance of the play. Then followed a grand and complicated shindy—one of those charming Parisian literary rows which excite the newspapers for days! In the end it was settled that neither M. de Noussanne's version nor any other version of "Les Polichinelles" should ever be produced, but that the journal *L'Illustration,* which gives away the text of a new play as a supplement about twice a month, should give, one week, Becque's original incomplete version exactly as it stands, and M. de Noussanne's completed version the next week, to the end that "the public might judge." Then Stock, the publisher, came along and sought to prevent the publication on the strength of a contract by which Becque had bound himself to give Stock his next play. (Times change, but not publishers!) However, *L'Illustration,* being wealthy and powerful, rode over M. Stock. And the amateurs of Becque have duly had the pleasure of reading "Les Polichinelles." Just as "Les Corbeaux" was the result of experiences gained in a domestic smash-up, and "La Parisienne" the result of experiences gained in a feverish liason, so

"Les Polichinelles" is the result of experiences gained on the Bourse. It is in five acts. The first two are practically complete, and they are exceedingly fine—quite equal to the very best Becque. The other acts are fragmentary, but some of the fragments are admirable. I can think of no living author who would be equal to the task of completing the play without making himself ridiculous. *20 Oct. '10*

Becque was unfortunate in death as in life. At his graveside, on the day of his funeral, his admirers said with one accord: "Every year on this day we will gather here. His name shall be a flag for us." But for several years they forgot all about Becque. And when at length they did come back, with a wreath, they could not find the grave. It was necessary to question keepers and to consult the official register of the cemetery. In the end the grave was re-discovered and everyone recognized it, and speeches were made, and the wreath piously deposited. The next year the admirers came again, with another wreath and more speeches. But some one had been before them. A wreath already lay on the grave; it bore this inscription: "To my dear husband

20 Oct. '10 defunct." Now Becque, though worried by liaisons, had lived and died a bachelor. The admirers had discoursed, the year before, at the grave of a humble clerk. After this Paris put up a statue to Becque. But it is only a bust. You can see it in the Avenue de Villiers.

HENRY JAMES

AT the beginning of this particularly active book season, reviewing the publishers' announcements, I wrote: "There are one or two promising items, including a novel by Henry James. And yet, honestly, am I likely at this time of day to be excited by a novel by Henry James? Shall I even read it? I know that I shall not. Still, I shall put it on my shelves, and tell my juniors what a miracle it is." Well, I have been surprised by the amount of resentment and anger which this honesty of mine has called forth. One of the politest of my correspondents, dating his letter from a city on the Rhine, says: "For myself, it's really a rotten shame; every week since 'Books and Persons' started have I hoped you would make some elucidating remarks on this wonderful writer's work, and now you don't even state why you propose not reading him!" And so on, with the result that when "The Finer Grain" (Methuen, 6s.) came along, I put my pride in my pocket, and read it. (By the way, it is not a novel but a collection of short stories, and I am pleased to see that it is candidly advertised as such.) I have never been an enthusiast *27 Oct. '10*

27 Oct. '10 for Henry James, and probably I have not read more than 25 per cent. of his entire output. The latest novel of his which I read was "The Ambassadors," and upon that I took oath I would never try another. I remember that I enjoyed "The Other House"; and that "In the Cage," a short novel about a post-office girl, delighted me. A few short stories have much pleased me. Beyond this, my memories of his work are vague. My estimate of Henry James might have been summed up thus: On the credit side:—He is a truly marvellous craftsman. By which I mean that he constructs with exquisite, never-failing skill, and that he writes like an angel. Even at his most mannered and his most exasperating, he conveys his meaning with more precision and clarity than perhaps any other living writer. He is never, never clumsy, nor dubious, even in the minutest details. Also he is a fine critic, of impeccable taste. Also he savours life with eagerness, sniffing the breeze of it like a hound . . . But on the debit side:—He is tremendously lacking in emotional power. Also his sense of beauty is over-sophisticated and wants originality. Also his attitude towards the spectacle of life is at bottom conventional, timid, and undecided. Also he seldom chooses themes of first-class importance, and when he does choose such a theme he never fairly bites it and makes it bleed. Also his curiosity is limited. He seems to me to have been specially created to be admired by super-dilettanti. (I do not say that to admire him is a proof of dilettantism.) What it all comes to is merely that his subject-matter does not as a rule interest me. I simply state my personal view, and I expressly assert my admiration for the craftsman in him and for the magnificent and consistent rectitude of his long artistic career. Further I will not go, though I know that bombs will now be laid at my front-door by the furious faithful. As for "The Finer Grain," it leaves me as I was —cold. It is an uneven collection, and the stories probably belong to different periods. The first, "The Velvet Glove," strikes me as conventional and without conviction. I should not call it subtle, but rather obvious. I should call it finicking. In the sentence-structure mannerism is pushed to excess. All the other stories are better. "Crafty Cornelia," for instance, is an exceedingly brilliant exercise in the art of making stone-soup. But then, I know I am in a minority *27 Oct. '10*

27 Oct. '10 among persons of taste. Some of the very best literary criticism of recent years has been aroused by admiration for Henry James. There is a man on the *Times Literary Supplement,* who, whenever he writes about Henry James, makes me feel that I have mistaken my vocation and ought to have entered the Indian Civil Service, or been a cattle-drover. However, I can't help it. And I give notice that I will not reply to scurrilous letters.

ENGLISH LITERARY CRITICISM

I LEARN that Mr. Elkin Mathews is about to publish a collected uniform edition of the works (poems and criticism) and correspondence of the late Lionel Johnson. I presume that this edition will comprise his study of Thomas Hardy. The enterprise proves that Lionel Johnson has admirers capable of an excellent piety; and it also argues a certain continuance of the demand for his books. I was never deeply impressed by Lionel Johnson's criticisms, and still less by his verse, but in the days of his activity I was young and difficult and hasty. Perhaps my net was too coarse for his fineness. But, anyhow, I would give much to have a large homogeneous body of English literary criticism to read *at*. And I should be obliged to anyone who would point out to me where such a body of first-rate criticism is to be found. I have never been able to find it for myself. When I think of Pierre Bayle, Ste. Beuve and Taine, and of the keen pleasure I derive from the immense pasture offered by their voluminous and consistently admirable works, I ask in vain where are the great English critics of *3 Nov. '10*

3 Nov. '10 English literature. Beside these French critics, the best of our own seem either fragmentary or provincial—yes, curiously provincial. Except Hazlitt we have, I believe, no even approximately first-class writer who devoted his main activity to criticism. And Hazlitt, though he is very readable, has neither the urbaneness, nor the science, nor the learning, nor the wide grasp of life and of history that characterizes the three above-named. Briefly, he didn't know enough.

Lamb would have been a first-class critic if he hadn't given the chief part of his life to clerkship. Lamb at any rate is not provincial. His perceptions are never at fault. Every sentence of Lamb proves his taste and his powerful intelligence. Coleridge—well, Coleridge has his comprehensible moments, but they are few; Matthew Arnold, with study and discipline, might perhaps have been a great critic, only his passion for literature was not strong enough to make him give up school-inspecting—and there you are! Moreover, Matthew Arnold could never have written of women as Ste. Beuve did. There were a lot of vastly interesting things that Matthew

Arnold did not understand and did not want to understand. He, too, was provincial (I regret to say)—you can feel it throughout his letters, though his letters make very good quiet reading. Churton Collins was a scholar of an extreme type; unfortunately he possessed no real feeling for literature, and thus his judgment, when it had to stand alone, cut a figure prodigiously absurd. And among living practitioners? Well, I have no hesitation in de-classing the whole professorial squad—Bradley, Herford, Dowden, Walter Raleigh, Elton, Saintsbury. The first business of any writer, and especially of any critical writer, is not to be mandarinic and tedious, and these lecturers have not yet learnt that first business. The best of them is George Saintsbury, but his style is such that even in Carmelite Street the sub-editors would try to correct it. Imagine the reception of such a style in Paris! Still, Professor Saintsbury does occasionally stray out of the university quadrangles, and puts on the semblance of a male human being as distinguished from an asexual pedagogue. Professor Walter Raleigh is improving. Professor Elton has never fallen to the depths of sterile and pretentious banality which are the natural and cus- *3 Nov. '10*

3 Nov. '10 tomary level of the remaining three. . . . You think I am letting my pen run away with me? Not at all. That is nothing to what I could say if I tried. Mr. J. W. Mackail might have been one of our major critics, but there again—he, too, prefers the security of a Government office, like Mr. Austin Dobson, who, by the way, is very good in a very limited sphere. Perhaps Austin Dobson is as good as we have. Compare his low flight with the terrific sweeping range of a Ste. Beuve or a Taine. I wish that some greatly gifted youth now aged about seventeen would make up his mind to be a literary critic and nothing else.

MRS. ELINOR GLYN

AFTER all, the world does move. I never thought to be able to congratulate the Circulating Libraries on their attitude towards a work of art; and here in common fairness I, who have so often animadverted upon their cowardice, am obliged to laud their courage. The instant cause of this is Mrs. Elinor Glyn's new novel, "His Hour" (Duckworths, 6s.) Everybody who cares for literature knows, or should know, Mrs. Glyn's fine carelessness of popular opinion (either here or in the States), and the singleness of her regard for the art which she practises and which she honours. Troubling herself about naught but splendour of subject and elevation of style, she goes on her career indifferent alike to the praise and to the blame of the mob. (I use the word "mob" in Fielding's sense—as meaning persons, in no matter what rank of life, capable of "low" feelings.) Perhaps Mrs. Glyn's latest book is the supreme example of her genius and of her conscientiousness. In essence it is a short story, handled with a fullness and a completeness which justify her in calling it a novel. There are two principal characters, a young half-Cossack *10 Nov. '10*

10 Nov. '10 Russian prince and an English widow of good family. The pet name of the former is "Gritzko." The latter is generally called Tamara. Gritzko is one of those heroic heroes who can spend their nights in the company of prostitutes, and their days in the solution of deep military problems. He is very wealthy; he has every attribute of a hero, including audacity. During their very first dance together Gritzko kissed Tamara. "They were up in a corner; everyone's back was turned to them happily, for in one second he had bent and kissed her neck. It was done with such incredible swiftness. . . ." etc. "But the kiss burnt into Tamara's flesh" . . . "'How dare you? How dare you?' she hissed."

Later ". . . 'I hate you!' almost hissed poor Tamara." (Note the realistic exactitude of that "almost.") "Then his eyes blazed. . . . He moved nearer to her, and spoke in a low concentrated voice: 'It is a challenge; good. Now listen to what I say: In a little short time you shall love me. That haughty little head shall be here on my breast without a struggle, and I shall kiss your lips until you cannot breathe.' For the second time in her life Tamara went dead white. . . ." Then follow scenes of revelry, in which Mrs. Glyn, with a courage as astonishing as her power, exposes all that is fatuous and vicious in the loftiest regions of Russian fashionable society. Later, Gritzko did kiss Tamara on the lips, but she objected. Still later he got the English widow in a lonely hut in a snowstorm, and this was "his hour." But she had a revolver. "'Touch me and I will shoot,' she gasped. . . . He made a step forward, but she lifted the pistol again to her head . . . and thus they glared at one another, the hunter and the hunted. . . . He flung himself on the couch and lit a cigarette, and all that was savage and cruel in him flamed from his eyes. 'My God! . . . and still I loved you—madly loved you . . . and last night when you defied me, then I determined you should belong to me by force. No power in heaven or earth can save you! Ah! If you had been different, how happy we might have been! But it is too late; the devil has won, and soon I will do what I please.' . . . For a long time there was silence. . . . Then the daylight faded quite, and the Prince got up and lit a small oil lamp. There was a deadly silence. . . . Ah! She must fight against this horrible lethargy. . . . Her *10 Nov. '10*

10 Nov. '10 arm had grown numb. . . . Strange lights seemed to flash before her eyes—yes—surely—that was Gritzko coming towards her! She gave a gasping cry and tried to pull the trigger, but it was stiff. . . . The pistol dropped from her nerveless grasp. . . . She gave one moan. . . . With a bound Gritzko leaped up. . . ."

"The light was gray when Tamara awoke. Where was she? What had happened? Something ghastly, but where? Then she perceived her torn blouse, and with a terrible pang remembrance came back to her. She started up, and as she did so realized that she was in her stockinged feet. The awful certainty. . . . Gritzko had won—she was utterly disgraced. . . . She hurriedly drew off the blouse, then she saw her torn underthings. . . . She knew that however she might make even the blouse look to the casual eyes of her godmother, she could never deceive her maid." . . . "She was an outcast. She was no better than Mary Gibson, whom Aunt Clara had with harshness turned out of the house. She—a lady!—a grand English lady! . . . She crouched down in a corner like a cowed dog. . . ." Then he wrote to her formally demanding her hand. And she replied: "To Prince Milaslavski. Monsieur,—I have no choice; I consent.—Yours truly, Tamara Loraine." Thus they were married. Her mood changed. "Oh! What did anything else matter in the world since after all he loved her! This beautiful fierce lover! Visions of enchantment presented themselves. . . . She buried her face in his scarlet coat. . . ." I must add that Gritzko had not really violated Tamara. He had only ripped open her corsage to facilitate respiration, and kissed her "little feet." She honestly thought herself the victim of a satyr; but, though she was a widow, with several years of marriage behind her, she had been quite mistaken on this point. You see, she was English. *10 Nov. '10*

"His Hour" is a sexual novel. It is magnificently sexual. My quotations, of course, do less than justice to it, but I think I have made clear the simple and highly courageous plot. Gritzko desired Tamara with the extreme of amorous passion, and in order to win her entirely he allowed her to believe that he had raped her. She, being an English widow, moving in the most refined circles, naturally regarded the outrage

10 Nov. '10 as an imperious reason for accepting his hand. That is a summary of Mrs. Glyn's novel, of which, by the way, I must quote the dedication: "With grateful homage and devotion I dedicate this book to Her Imperial Highness The Grand Duchess Vladimir of Russia. In memory of the happy evenings spent in her gracious presence when reading to her these pages, which her sympathetic aid in facilitating my opportunities for studying the Russian character enabled me to write. Her kind appreciation of the finished work is a source of the deepest gratification to me."

The source of the deepest gratification to me is the fact that the Censorship Committee of the United Circulating Libraries should have allowed this noble, daring, and masterly work to pass freely over their counters. What a change from January of this year, when Mary Gaunt's "The Uncounted Cost," which didn't show the ghost of a rape, could not even be advertised in the organ of The *Times* Book Club! After this, who can complain against a Library Censorship? It is true that while passing "His Hour," the same censorship puts its ban absolute upon Mr. John Trevena's new novel

"Bracken." It is true that quite a number of people had considered Mr. Trevena to be a serious and dignified artist of rather considerable talent. It is true that "Bracken" probably contains nothing that for sheer brave sexuality can be compared with a score of passages in "His Hour." What then? The Censorship Committee must justify its existence somehow. Mr. Trevena ought to have dedicated his wretched provincial novel to the Queen of Montenegro. He painfully lacks "savoir-vivre." In the early part of this year certain mysterious meetings took place apropos of the Censorship, between a sub-committee of the Society of Authors and a sub-committee of the Publishers' Association. But nothing was done. I am told that the Authors' Society is now about to take the matter up again. But why? *10 Nov. '10*

W. H. HUDSON

24 Nov. '10 I SUPPOSE that there are few writers less "literary" than Mr. W. H. Hudson, and few among the living more likely to be regarded, a hundred years hence, as having produced "literature." He is so unassuming, so mild, so intensely and unconsciously original in the expression of his naïve emotions before the spectacle of life, that a hasty inquirer into his idiosyncrasy might be excused for entirely missing the point of him. His new book (which helps to redeem the enormous vulgarity of a booming season), "A Shepherd's Life: Impressions of the South Wiltshire Downs" (Methuens), is soberly of a piece with his long and deliberate career. A large volume, yet one arrives at the end of it with surprising quickness, because the pages seem to slip over of themselves. Everything connected with the Wiltshire downs is in it, together with a good deal not immediately therewith connected. For example, Mr. Hudson's views on primary education, which are not as mature as his views about shepherds and wild beasts of the downs. He seldom omits to describe the individualities of the wild beasts of his acquaintance. For him a mole is not any mole, but a particular mole. He will tell you about a mole that did not dig like other moles but had a method of its own, and he will give you the reason why this singular mole lived to a great age. As a rule, he remarks with a certain sadness, wild animals die prematurely, their existence being exciting and dangerous. How many men know England—I mean the actual earth and flesh that make England—as Mr. Hudson knows it? This is his twelfth book, and four or five of the dozen are already classics. Probably no literary dining club or association of authors or journalists male or female will ever give a banquet in Mr. Hudson's honour. It would not occur to the busy organizers of these affairs to do so. And yet—— But, after all, it is well that he should be spared such an ordeal. *24 Nov. '10*

NEO-IMPRESSIONISM AND LITERATURE

8 Dec. '10 THE exhibition of the so-called "Neo-Impressionists" over which the culture of London is now laughing, has an interest which is perhaps not confined to the art of painting. For me, personally, it has a slight, vague repercussion upon literature. The attitude of the culture of London towards it is of course merely humiliating to any Englishman who has made an effort to cure himself of insularity. It is one more proof that the negligent disdain of Continental artists for English artistic opinion is fairly well founded. The mild tragedy of the thing is that London is infinitely too self-complacent even to suspect that it is London and not the exhibition which is making itself ridiculous. The laughter of London in this connexion is just as silly, just as provincial, just as obtuse, as would be the laughter of a small provincial town were Strauss's "Salome," or Debussy's "Pelléas et Mélisande" offered for its judgment. One can imagine the shocked, contemptuous resentment of a London musical amateur (one of those that arrived at Covent Garden box-office at 6 a.m. the other day to secure a seat for "Salome") at the guffaw of a provincial town confronted by the spectacle and the noise of the famous "Salome" osculation. But the amusement of that same amateur confronted by an uncompromizing "Neo-Impressionist" picture amounts to exactly the same guffaw. The guffaw is legal. You may guffaw before Rembrandt (people do!), but in so doing you only add to the sum of human stupidity. London may be unaware that the value of the best work of this new school is permanently and definitely settled—outside London. So much the worse for London. For the movement has not only got past the guffaw stage; it has got past the arguing stage. Its authenticity is admitted by all those who have kept themselves fully awake. And in twenty years London will be signing an apology for its guffaw. It will be writing itself down an ass. The writing will consist of large cheques payable for Neo-Impressionist pictures to Messrs. Christie Manson and Woods. London is already familiar with this experience, and doesn't mind. *8 Dec. '10*

Who am I that I should take exception to the guffaw? Ten years ago I too guffawed,

8 Dec. '10 though I hope with not quite the Kensingtonian twang. The first Cézannes I ever saw seemed to me to be very funny. They did not disturb my dreams, because I was not in the business. But my notion about Cézanne was that he was a fond old man who distracted himself by daubing. I could not say how my conversion to Cézanne began. When one is not a practising expert in an art, a single word, a single intonation, uttered by an expert whom one esteems, may commence a process of change which afterwards seems to go on by itself. But I remember being very much impressed by a still-life—some fruit in a bowl—and on approaching it I saw Cézanne's clumsy signature in the corner. From that moment the revelation was swift. And before I had seen any Gauguins at all, I was prepared to consider Gauguin with sympathy. The others followed naturally. I now surround myself with large photographs of these pictures of which a dozen years ago I was certainly quite incapable of perceiving the beauty. The best still-life studies of Cézanne seem to me to have the grandiose quality of epics. And that picture by Gauguin, showing the back of a Tahitian young man with a Tahitian girl on either

side of him, is an affair which I regard with acute pleasure every morning. There are compositions by Vuillard which equally enchant me. Naturally I cannot accept the whole school—no more than the whole of any school. I have derived very little pleasure from Matisse, and the later developments of Félix Vallotton leave me in the main unmoved. But one of the very latest phenomena of the school—the water-colours of Pierre Laprade—I have found ravishing. *8 Dec. '10*

It is in talking to several of these painters, in watching their familiar deportment, and particularly in listening to their conversations with others on subjects other than painting, that I have come to connect their ideas with literature. They are not good theorizers about art; and I am not myself a good theorizer about art; a creative artist rarely is. But they do ultimately put their ideas into words. You may receive one word one day and the next next week, but in the end an idea gets itself somehow stated. Whenever I have listened to Laprade criticizing pictures, especially students' work, I have thought about literature; I have been forced to wonder whether I should

8 Dec. '10 not have to reconsider my ideals. The fact is that some of these men are persuasive in themselves. They disengage, in their talk, in their profound seriousness, in their sense of humour, in the sound organization of their industry, and in their calm assurance—they disengage a convincingness that is powerful beyond debate. An artist who is truly original cannot comment on boot-laces without illustrating his philosophy and consolidating his position. Noting in myself that a regular contemplation of these pictures inspires a weariness of all other pictures that are not absolutely first-rate, giving them a disconcerting affinity to the tops of chocolate-boxes or to "art" photographs, I have permitted myself to suspect that supposing some writer were to come along and do in words what these men have done in paint, I might conceivably be disgusted with nearly the whole of modern fiction, and I might have to begin again. This awkward experience will in all probability not happen to me, but it might happen to a writer younger than me. At any rate it is a fine thought. The average critic always calls me, both in praise and dispraise, "photographic"; and I always rebut the epithet with disdain, because in the sense meant by the average critic I am not photographic. But supposing that in a deeper sense I were? Supposing a young writer turned up and forced me, and some of my contemporaries—us who fancy ourselves a bit—to admit that we had been concerning ourselves unduly with inessentials, that we had been worrying ourselves to achieve infantile realisms? Well, that day would be a great and a disturbing day—for us. *8 Dec. '10*

1911

BOOKS OF THE YEAR

THE practice of reviewing the literature of the year at the end thereof is now decaying. Newspapers still give a masterly survey of the motor cars of the year. I remember the time when it was part of my duty as a serious journalist to finish at Christmas a two-thousand word article, full of discrimination as fine as Irish lace, about the fiction of the year; and other terrifying specialists were engaged to deal amply with the remaining branches of literature. To-day, one man in one column and one day will polish off what five of us scarcely exhausted in seven columns and seven days. I am referring to the distant past of a dozen years ago, before William de Morgan was born, and before America and Elinor Glyn had discovered each other. Last week many newspapers dismissed the entire fiction of 1910 in a single paragraph. The consequence is that there has been no "book of the year." A critic without space to spread himself hesitates to pronounce downright for a particular book. A critic engaged in the dangerous art of creating the "book of the year" wants room to hedge, and in the newest journalism there is no room to hedge. *12 Jan. '11*

12 Jan. '11 So the critic refrains from the act of creation. He imitates the discretion of the sporting tipster, who names several horses as being likely to win one race. "Among the books of the year are Blank, Blank and Blank," he says. (But what he means is, "The book of the year is to be found among Blank, Blank and Blank.") Naturally he selects among the books whose titles come into his head with the least difficulty; that is to say, the books which he has most recently reviewed; that is to say, the books published during the autumn season. No doubt during the spring season he has distinguished several books as being "great," "masterly," "unforgettable," "genius"; but ere the fall of the leaf these works have completely escaped from his memory. No author, and particularly no novelist who wishes to go down to posterity, should publish during the spring season; it is fatal.

The celebrated "Dop Doctor" (published by Heinemann) and Mr. Temple Thurston's "City of Beautiful Nonsense" (published by Chapman and Hall) have both sold very well indeed throughout the entire year. In fact, they were selling better in December than many successful novels published in the autumn. Yet neither of them, assuming that there had been a book of the year, would have had much chance of being that book. The reason is that they have not been sufficiently "talked about." I mean "talked about" by "the right people." And by "right people" I mean the people who make a practice of dining out at least three times a week in the West End of London to the accompaniment of cultured conversation. I mean the people who are "in the know," politically, socially, and intellectually—who know what Mr. F. E. Smith says to Mr. Winston Churchill in private, why Mrs. Humphry Ward made such an enormous pother at the last council meeting of the Authors' Society, what is really the matter with Mr. Bernard Shaw's later work, whether Mr. Balfour does indeed help Mr. Garvin to write the *Daily Telegraph* leaders, and whether the Savoy Restaurant is as good under the new management as under the old. I reckon there are about 12,055 of these people. They constitute the *élite*. Without their aid, without their refined and judicial twittering, no book can hope to be a book of the year. *12 Jan. '11*

12 Jan. '11 Now I am in a position to state that no novel for very many years has been so discussed by the *élite* as Mr. Forster's "Howard's End" (published by Edward Arnold). The ordinary library reader knows that it has been a very considerable popular success; persons of genuine taste know that it is a very considerable literary achievement; but its triumph is that it has been mightily argued about during the repasts of the *élite*. I need scarcely say that it is not Mr. Forster's best book; no author's best book is ever the best received—this is a rule practically without exception. A more curious point about it is that it contains a lot of very straight criticism of the *élite*. And yet this point is not very curious either. For the *élite* have no objection whatever to being criticized. They rather like it, as the alligator likes being tickled with peas out of a pea-shooter. Their hides are superbly impenetrable. And I know not which to admire the more, the American's sensitiveness to pea-shooting, or the truly correct Englishman's indestructible indifference to it. Mr. Forster is a young man. I believe he is still under thirty, if not under twenty-nine. If he continues to write one book a year regularly, to be discreet and mysterious, to refrain absolutely from certain themes, and to avoid a too marked tendency to humour, he will be the most fashionable novelist in England in ten years time. His worldly prospects are very brilliant indeed. If, on the other hand, he writes solely to please himself, forgetting utterly the existence of the *élite,* he may produce some first-class literature. The responsibilities lying upon him at this crisis of his career are terrific. And he so young too! *12 Jan. '11*

"THE NEW MACHIAVELLI"

2 Feb. '11 A PRETTY general realization of the extremely high quality of "The New Machiavelli" has reduced almost to silence the ignoble tittle-tattle that accompanied its serial publication in the *English Review*. It is years since a novel gave rise to so much offensive and ridiculous chatter before being issued as a book. When the chatter began, dozens of people who would no more dream of paying four-and-sixpence for a new novel that happened to be literature than they would dream of paying four-and-sixpence for a cigar, sent down to the offices of the *English Review* for complete sets of back numbers at half-a-crown a number, so that they could rummage without a moment's delay among the earlier chapters in search of tit-bits according to their singular appetite. Such was the London which calls itself literary and political! A spectacle to encourage cynicism! Rumour had a wonderful time. It was stated that not only the libraries but the booksellers also would decline to handle "The New Machiavelli." The reasons for this prophesied ostracism were perhaps vague, but they were understood to be broad-based upon the unprecedented audacity of the novel. And really in this exciting year, with Sir Percy Bunting in charge of the national sense of decency, and Mr. W. T. Stead still gloating after twenty-five years over his success in keeping Sir Charles Dilke out of office—you never can tell what may happen! *2 Feb. '11*

However, it is all over now. "The New Machiavelli" has been received with the respect and with the enthusiasm which its tremendous qualities deserve. It is a great success. And the reviews have on the whole been generous. It was perhaps not to be expected that certain Radical dailies should swallow the entire violent dose of the book without kicking up a fuss; but, indeed, Mr. Scott James, in the *Daily News,* ought to know better than to go running about after autobiography in fiction. The human nose was not designed by an all-merciful providence for this purpose. Mr. Scott James has undoubted gifts as a critic, and his temperament is sympathetic; and the men most capable of appreciating him, and whose appreciation he would probably like to retain, would esteem him even more highly if he could get into his head the simple fact that a novel is a novel. I have suffered

2 Feb. '11 myself from this very provincial mania for chemically testing novels for traces of autobiography. There are some critics of fiction who talk about autobiography in fiction in the tone of a doctor who has found arsenic in the stomach at a post-mortem inquiry. The truth is that whenever a scene in a novel is *really* convincing, a certain type of critical and uncreative mind will infallibly mutter in accents of pain, "Autobiography!" When I was discussing this topic the other day a novelist not inferior to Mr. Wells suddenly exclaimed: "I say! Supposing we *did* write autobiography!" . . . Yes, if we did, what a celestial rumpus there would be!

The carping at "The New Machiavelli" is naught. For myself I anticipated for it a vast deal more carping than it has in fact occasioned. And I am very content to observe a marked increase of generosity in the reception of Mr. Wells' work. To me the welcome accorded to his best books has always seemed to lack spontaneity, to be characterized by a mean reluctance. And yet if there is a novelist writing to-day who by generosity has deserved generosity, that novelist is H. G. Wells. Astounding width of observation; a marvellously true perspective; an extraordinary grasp of the real significance of innumerable phenomena utterly diverse; profound emotional power; dazzling verbal skill: these are qualities which Mr. Wells indubitably has. But the qualities which consecrate these other qualities are his priceless and total sincerity, and the splendid human generosity which colours that sincerity. What above all else we want in this island of intellectual dishonesty is someone who will tell us the truth "and chance it." H. G. Wells is pre-eminently that man. He might have told us the truth with cynicism; he might have told it meanly; he might have told it tediously—and he would still have been invaluable. But it does just happen that he has combined a disconcerting and entrancing candour with a warmth of generosity towards mankind and an inspiring faith in mankind such as no other living writer, not even the most sentimental, has surpassed. And yet in the immediate past we have heard journalists pronouncing coldly: "This thing is not so bad." And we have heard journalists asserting in tones of shocked reprehension: "This thing is not free from faults!" Who the deuce said it was free

2 Feb. '11

2 Feb. '11 from faults? But where in fiction, ancient or modern, will you find another philosophical picture of a whole epoch and society as brilliant and as honest as "The New Machiavelli"? Well, I will tell you where you will find it. You will find it in "Tono-Bungay." H. G. Wells is a bit of sheer luck for England. Some countries don't know their luck. And as I do not believe that England is worse than another, I will say that no country knows its luck. However, as regards this particular bit, there are now some clear signs of a growing perception.

The social and political questions raised in "The New Machiavelli" might be discussed at length with great advantage. But this province is not mine. Nor could the rightness or the wrongness of the hero's views and acts affect the artistic value of the novel. On purely artistic grounds the novel might be criticized in several ways unfavourably. But in my opinion it has only one fault that to any appreciable extent impairs its artistic worth. The politically-creative part, as distinguished from the politically-shattering part, is not convincing. The hero's change of party, and his popular success with the policy of the endowment of motherhood are indeed strangely unconvincing—inconceivable to commonsense. Here the author's hand has trembled, and his persuasive power forsaken him. Happily he recaptured it for the final catastrophe, which is absolutely magnificent, a masterpiece of unforced poignant tragedy and unsentimental tenderness. *2 Feb. '11*

SUCCESS IN JOURNALISM

16 Feb. '11 It is notorious that in London—happily so different from other capitals—there is no connexion between the advertisement and the editorial departments of the daily papers. It is positively known, for instance, that the exuberant editorial praise poured out upon the new "Encyclopædia Britannica" has no connexion whatever with the tremendous sums paid by the Cambridge University Press for advertising the said work of reference. The almost simultaneous appearance of the advertisements and of the superlative reviews is a pure coincidence. Now, in Paris it would not be a coincidence, and nobody would have the courage to pretend that it was. But London is a city apart. In view of this admitted fact I was intensely startled, not to say outraged, by a conversation at which I assisted the other day. A young acquaintance, with literary and journalistic proclivities, and with a touching belief in the high mission of the London press, desired advice as to the best method of reaching the top rungs of the ladder of which he had not yet set foot even on the lowest rung. I therefore invited him to meet a celebrated friend of mine, an author and a journalist, who has recently quitted an important editorial chair. *16 Feb. '11*

The latter spoke to him as follows: "My dear boy, you had better get a situation in the advertisement department of a paper—no matter what paper, provided it has a large advertisement revenue; and no matter what situation, however modest." Here the youth interrupted with the remark that his desire was the editorial department. The ex-editor proceeded calmly: "I have quite grasped that. . . . Well, you must work yourself up in the advertisement department! What you chiefly require for success is a good suit, a good club, an imperturbable manner, and a cultivated taste in restaurants and bars. In your spare time you must write long dull articles for the reviews; and you must re-discover London in a series of snappish sketches for a half-penny daily, and also write a novel that is just true enough to frighten the libraries and not too true to make them refuse it altogether: it must absolutely be such a novel as they will supply only to such subscribers as insist on having it. When you have worked your way very high up in the advertisement department, and are intimate with advertisement agents

16 Feb. '11 and large advertisers to the point of being able to influence advertisements amounting to fifty thousand pounds a year—then, and not before, you may look about you and decide what big serious daily paper you would like to assist in editing. Make your own choice. Then see the proprietor. If he is not already in the House of Lords, he will assuredly be on Mr. Asquith's private list of five hundred candidates for the House of Lords. The best moment to catch him is as he comes out of the Palace Theatre, about a quarter past eleven of a night. Tell him on the pavement that you have edited a paper in Chicago, and he will at once invite you into his automobile. You go with him to his club, and then you confess that you have not edited a paper in Chicago, but that you have adopted this device in order to get speech with him, and that all you desire is a humble post on the editorial staff of his big serious daily.

"He will insult you. He will inform you that he has forty candidates for the most insignificant post on the editorial staff, and that there is not the remotest chance for you. You then tell him that you are an expert writer, a contributor to the monthlies and quarterlies, and the author of a novel which Mr. James Douglas has described as the most stupendously virile work of fiction since Turgeneff's 'Crime and Punishment.' He will insult you anew, and demand your immediate departure. You then say to him, in a casual tone: 'I can bring you ten thousand pounds' worth of ads. a year.' He will read your deepest soul with one glance, and will reply, in a casual tone, 'I daresay I could find you something regular to do on the magazine page.' You go on airily: 'I'm pretty sure I can bring twenty thousand pounds' worth of ads. a year.' He will then order R.P. Muria cigars, and say with benevolence: 'It just happens that the head of our reviewing department is under notice. How would that suit you?' You then unmask all your batteries, and tell him squarely that you can bring him advertisements to the tune of a thousand pounds a week. Whereupon he will reply, shaking you fraternally by the hand: 'My dear fellow, I will make you editor at once.'" *16 Feb. '11*

So spake my celebrated friend. Of course, he is a cynic. He may be a criminal cynic. But he spake so. From time to time London dailies do me the honour to reprint

16 Feb. '11 saucy paragraphs from this weekly article of mine. My friend said to me: "You can print what I've said, if you like. No daily paper in London will reprint *that*."

MARGUERITE AUDOUX

AMONG the astonishing phenomena of a spring season which promises to be quite as successful, in its way, as the very glorious autumn season (publishers must have spent a happy Christmas!) is the success of a really distinguished book. I mean "Marie Claire." Frankly, I did not anticipate this triumph. For, of course, it is very difficult for an author of experience to believe that a good book will be well received. However, "Marie Claire" has been helped by a series of extraordinary reviews. No novel of recent years has had such favourable reviews, or so many of them, or such long ones. I have seen all of them—all except one have been very laudatory—and I am in a position to state that if placed end to end they would stretch from Miss Corelli's house in Stratford-on-Avon across the main to Mr. Hall Caine's castle in the Isle of Man. This may be called praise. One of the best, if not the best, was signed "J. L. G." in the *Observer*. It is indeed a solemn and terrifying thought that Mr. Garvin, who, by means of thoroughly bad prose persisted in during many years, has at last laid the Tory Party in ruins, should be so excellent a judge of literature. *2 March '11*

2 March '11 Mr. Garvin made his début in the London Press, I think, as a literary critic; and it is a pity (from the Tory point of view) that he did not remain a literary critic. I am convinced that Mr. Balfour and Lord Lansdowne would personally subscribe large sums to found a literary paper for him to edit, on condition that he promised never to write another line of advice to their party. The *Telegraph* would bleed copiously; the *Observer* would expire; the *Fortnightly Review* would stagger in its heavy stride, but there would be hope for Tories! . . . In the meantime, five thousand copies of the English translation of "Marie Claire" were sold within a week of publication. It is improbable that the total English sale will be less than ten thousand. Now translated novels rarely achieve popularity. The last one to be popular here was Fogazzaro's "The Saint"; but the popularity of "The Saint" was not due to artistic causes.

I think I may say that I am thoroughly accustomed to the society of women-novelists. Peculiar circumstances in my obscure life have thrown me among women-writers of all sorts; and I can boast that I have helped to form more than one woman-novelist; so that the prospect of meeting a new one does not agitate me in the slightest degree. I make friends with the new one at once, and in about two minutes we are discussing prices with the most touching familiarity. Nevertheless, I own that I was somewhat disturbed in my Midland phlegm when the author of "Marie Claire" came to see me. The book, read in the light of the circumstances of its composition, had unusually impressed me and stirred my imagination. It was not the woman-novelist who was coming to see me, but Marie Claire herself, shepherdess, farm-servant, and sempstress; it was a mysterious creature who had known how to excite enthusiasm in a whole regiment of literary young men. . . . And literary young men as a rule are extremely harsh, even offensive, in their attitude towards women-writers. I stood at the top of the toy-stairs of the *pavillon* which I was then occupying in Paris, and Madame Marguerite Audoux came up the stairs towards me, preceded by one of her young sponsors, and followed by another. A rather short, plump little lady, very simply dressed, and with the simplest possible manner—just such a comfortable human being as in my part of the world is *2 March '11*

2 March '11 called a "body"! She had, however, eyes of a softness and depth such as are not seen in my part of the world. With that, a very quiet, timid, and sweet voice. She was a sempstress; she looked like a sempstress; and she was well content to look like a sempstress. Nobody would have guessed in ten thousand guesses that here was the author of the European book of the year. But when she talked the resemblance to the sempstress soon vanished. Sempstresses—of whom I have also known many—do not talk as she talked. Not that she said much! Not that she began to talk at once! Far from it. When I had referred to the goodness of her visit, and she had referred to the goodness of my invitation, and she was ensconced in an arm-chair near the fire, she quite simply left the pioneer work of conversation to her bodyguard. Her bodyguard was very proud, and very nervous, as befitted its age.

It was my reference to Dostoievsky that first started her talking. In all literary conversations Dostoievsky is my King Charles's head. She had previously stated that she had read very little indeed. But at any rate she had read Dostoievsky, and was well minded to share my enthusiasms. Indeed, Dostoievsky drew her out of her arm-chair and right across the room. We were soon discussing methods of work, and I learnt that she worked very slowly indeed, destroying much, and feeling her way inch by inch rather than seeing it clear ahead. She said that her second book, dealing with her life in Paris, might not be ready for years. It was evident that she profoundly understood the nature of work—all sorts of work. Work had, indeed, left its honourable and fine mark upon her. She made some very subtle observations about the psychology of it, but unfortunately I cannot adequately report them here. . . . From work to prices, naturally! It was pleasing to find that she had a very sane and proper curiosity as to prices and conditions in England. After I had somewhat satisfied this curiosity she showed an equally sane and proper annoyance at the fact that the English and American rights of "Marie Claire" had been sold outright for a ridiculous sum. She told me the exact sum. It was either £16 or £20—I forget which. *2 March '11*

When Madame Audoux had gone I reviewed my notions of her visit, and I came

2 March '11 to the conclusion that she was very like her book. She had said little, and nothing that was striking, but she had mysteriously emanated an atmosphere of artistic distinction. She was a true sensitive. She had had immense and deep experience of life, but her adventures, often difficult, had not disturbed the nice balance of her judgment, nor impaired the delicacy of her impressions. She was an amateur of life. She was awake to all aspects of it. And a calm commonsense presided over her magnanimous verdicts. She was far too wary, sagacious, and well acquainted with real values to allow herself to be spoilt, even the least bit, by a perilous success, however brilliant. Such were my notions. But it is not in a single interview that one can arrive at a due estimate of a mind so reserved, dreamy, and complex as hers. The next day she left Paris, and I have not seen her since.

JOHN MASEFIELD

I OPENED Mr. John Masefield's novel of modern London, "The Street of To-day" (Dent and Co.), with much interest. But I found it very difficult to read. This is a damning criticism; but what would you have? I found it very difficult to read. It is very earnest, very sincere, very carefully and generously done. But these qualities will not save it. Even its intelligence, and its alert critical attitude towards life, will not save it. I could say a great deal of good about it, and yet all that I could say in its favour would not avail. It would certainly be better if it were considerably shorter. I estimate that between fifty and a hundred pages of small talk and miscellaneous observation could be safely removed from it without impairing the coherence of the story. The amount of small talk recorded is simply terrific. Not bad small talk! Heard in real life, it would be reckoned rather good small talk! But artistically futile! Small talk, and cleverer small talk than this, smothered and ruined a novel more dramatic than this—I mean Mr. Zangwill's "The Master." I am convinced that a novel ought to be dramatic— *20 April '11*

20 April '11 intellectually, spiritually, or physically—and "The Street of To-day" is not dramatic. It is always about to be dramatic and it never is. Chapter III, for instance, contains very important material, essential to the tale, fundamental. But it is not presented dramatically. It is presented in the form of a psychological essay. Now Mr. Masefield's business as a novelist was to have invented happenings for the presentment of the information contained in this essay. He has saved himself a lot of trouble, but to my mind he has not yet come to understand what a novel is.

His creative power is not yet mature. That is to say, he does not convince the reader in the measure which one would expect from a writer of his undoubted emotional faculty. And yet he is often guilty of carelessness in corroborative detail—such carelessness as only a mighty tyrant over the reader could afford. The story deals largely with journalism. And one of the papers most frequently mentioned is "The Backwash." Now no paper could possibly be called "The Backwash." It is conceivable that a paper might be called "The Tip Top." It is just conceivable that a paper might be called "Snip Snap." But "The Backwash," never! Mr. Masefield knows this as well as anybody. The aim of his nomenclature was obviously satiric—an old dodge which did very well in the loose Victorian days, but which is excruciatingly out of place in a modern strictly-realistic novel. A trifle, you say! Not at all! Every time "The Backwash" is mentioned, the reader thinks: "No paper called 'The Backwash' ever existed." And a fresh break is made in Mr. Masefield's convincingness. A modern novelist may not permit himself these freakish negligences. Another instance of the same fault is the Christian name of Mrs. Bailey in "The New Machiavelli." It was immensely clever of Mr. Wells to christen her "Altiora." But in so doing he marred the extraordinary brilliance of his picture of her. If you insist that I am talking about trifles, I can only insist that a work of art is a series of trifles. *20 April '11*

Mr. Masefield's style suffers in a singular manner. It is elaborate in workmanship—perhaps to the point of an excessive self-consciousness. But its virtue is constantly being undermined by inexactitudes which irritate and produce doubt. For example:

20 April '11 "They entered the tube station. In the train they could not talk much. Lionel kept his brain alert with surmise as to the character of the passengers. Like Blake, a century before, he found 'marks of weakness, marks of woe,' on each face there." Blake in the tube! Mr. Masefield will produce a much better novel than "The Street of To-day."

LECTURES AND STATE PERFORMANCES

DRIVEN by curiosity I went to hear Mr. H. G. Wells' lecture last Thursday at the Times Book Club on "The Scope of the Novel." Despite the physical conditions of heat and noise, and an open window exactly behind the lecturer (whose voice thus flowed just as much into a back street as into the ears of his auditors), the affair was a success, and it is to be hoped that the Times Book Club will pursue the enterprise further. It was indeed a remarkable phenomenon: a first-class artist speaking the truth about fiction to a crowd of circulating-library subscribers! Mr. Wells was above all defiant; he contrived to put in some very plain speaking about Thackeray, and he finished by asserting that it was futile for the fashionable public to murmur against the intellectual demands of the best modern fiction,—there was going to be no change unless it might be a change in the direction of the more severe, the more candid, and the more exhaustively curious. *25 May '11*

Of course the lecturer had to vulgarise his messages so as to get them safely into the

25 May '11 brain of the audience. What an audience! For the first time in my life I saw the "library" public in the mass! It is a sight to make one think. My cab had gone up Bond Street where the fortune-tellers flourish, and their flags wave in the wind, and their painted white hands point alluringly up mysterious staircases. These fortune-tellers make a tolerable deal of money, and the money they make must come out chiefly of the pockets of well-dressed library subscribers. Not a doubt but that many of Mr. Wells' audience were clients of the soothsayers. A strange multitude! It appeared to consist of a thousand women and Mr. Bernard Shaw. Women deemed to be elegant, women certainly deeming themselves to be elegant! I, being far from the rostrum, had a good view of the backs of their blouses, chemisettes and bodices. What an assortment of pretentious and ill-made toilettes! What disclosures of clumsy hooks-and-eyes and general creased carelessness! It would not do for me to behold the "library" public in the mass too often!

I could not but think of the State performance of "Money" at Drury Lane on the previous night: that amusing smack at living artists. There has been a good deal of straight talk about it in the daily and weekly papers. But the psychology of the matter has not been satisfactorily explained. Blame has been laid at the King's door. I think wrongly, or at least unfairly. Besides being one of the two best shots in the United Kingdom, the King is beyond any question a man of honourable intentions and of a strict conscientiousness. But it is no part of his business to be sufficiently expert to choose a play for a State performance. He has never pretended to have artistic proclivities. Who among you, indeed, could be relied upon to choose properly a play for a State performance? Take the best modern plays. Who among you would dare to suggest for a State performance Oscar Wilde's "The Importance of Being Earnest," Bernard Shaw's "Man and Superman," John Galsworthy's "Justice," or Granville Barker's "The Voysey Inheritance"? Nobody! These plays are unthinkable for a State performance, because their distinction is utterly beyond the average comprehension of the ruling classes,—and State performances are for the ruling classes. These plays are simply too good. Yet if you don't choose an old play you *25 May '11*

25 May '11 must choose one of these four plays, or make the worst of both worlds. Modern plays being ruled out, you must either have Shakespeare or—or what? What is there? "The Cenci"?

Can you not now sympathize with the King as he ran through, in his mind, the whole range of British drama? But the truth is that he did not run through the whole range of British drama. Invariably in these cases a list is submitted for the sovereign to choose from. It is an open secret that in this particular case such a list was prepared. Whether or not it was prepared by Mr. Arthur Collins, organizer of Drury Lane pantomimes, I cannot say. The list contained Shakespeare and Lytton, and I don't know who else. Conceivably the King did not want Shakespeare. To my mind he would be quite justified in not wanting Shakespeare. We are glutted with Shakespeare in the Haymarket. Well, then, —why not "Money"? It is a famous play. We all know its name and the name of its author. And that is the limit of our knowledge. Why should the King be supposed to be acquainted with its extreme badness? I confess I didn't know it was so bad as now it seems to be. And, not very long ago, was not Sir William Robertson Nicoll defending the genius of Lytton in the *British Weekly?* It is now richly apparent that "Money" ought not to have been included in the list submitted to the King. But it is easy to be wise after the event. *25 May '11*

Let it be for ever understood that State theatres and State performances never have had, never will have, any real connexion with original dramatic art. That is one reason why I am against a national theatre, whose influence on the drama is bound to be sinister. To count the performance of "Money" as an insult to living artists is to lose sight of a main factor in the case. The State and living art must be mutually opposed, for the reason that the State must, and quite rightly does, represent the average of opinion. For an original artist to expect aid from the State is silly; it is also wrong. In expressing a particular regard for the feelings of musical comedy, and in announcing beforehand his intention of being present at the first night of the new Gaiety masterpiece, the King was properly fulfilling his

25 May '11 duties as a monarch towards dramatic art. Art is not the whole of life, and to adore musical comedy is not a crime. The best thing original artists can do is to keep their perspective undistorted.

A PLAY OF TCHEHKOFF'S

AT last, thanks to the Stage Society, we have had a good representative play of Anton Tchehkoff on the London stage. Needless to say, Tchehkoff was done in the provinces long ago. "The Cherry Orchard," I have been told, is Tchehkoff's dramatic masterpiece, and I can well believe it. But it is a dangerous thing to present foreign masterpieces to a West End audience, and the directors of the Stage Society discovered, or re-discovered, this fact on Sunday night last. The reception of "The Cherry Orchard" was something like what the reception of Ibsen's plays used to be twenty years ago. It was scarcely even a mixed reception. There could be no mistake about the failure of the play to please the vast majority of the members of the Society. At the end of the second act signs of disapproval were very manifest indeed, and the exodus from the theatre began. A competent authority informed me that at the end of the third act half the audience had departed; but in the narrative fever of the moment the competent authority may have slightly exaggerated. Certain it is that multitudes preferred Aldwych and the *8 June '11*

8 June '11 restaurant-concerts, or even their own homes, to Tchehkoff's play. And as the evening was the Sabbath you may judge the extreme degree of their detestation of the play.

A director of the Stage Society said to me on the Monday: "If our people won't stand it, it has no chance, because we have the pick here." I didn't contradict him, but I by no means agreed that he had the pick there. The managing committee of the Society is a very enlightened body; but the mass of the members is just as stupid as any other mass. Its virtue is that it pays subscriptions, thus enabling the committee to make experiments and to place before the forty or fifty persons in London who really can judge a play the sort of play which is worthy of curiosity.

In spite of the antipathy which is aroused, "The Cherry Orchard" is quite inoffensive. For example, there is nothing in it to which the Censor could possibly object. It does not deal specially with sex. It presents an average picture of Russian society. But it presents the picture with such exact, uncomprising truthfulness that the members of the Stage Society mistook nearly all the portraits for caricatures, and tedious caricatures. In naturalism the play is assuredly an advance on any other play that I have seen or that has been seen in England. Its naturalism is positively daring. The author never hesitates to make his personages as ridiculous as in life they would be. In this he differs from every other playwright that I know of. Ibsen, for instance; and Henri Becque. He has carried an artistic convention much nearer to reality, and achieved another step in the evolution of the drama. The consequence is that he is accused of untruth and exaggeration, as Becque was, as Ibsen was. His truthfulness frightens, and causes resentment. *8 June '11*

People say: "No such persons exist, or at any rate such persons are too exceptional to form proper material for a work of art." No such persons, I admit, exist in England; but then this play happens to be concerned with Russia, and even the men's costumes in it are appalling. Moreover, persons equally ridiculous and futile do exist in England, and by the hundred thousand; only they are ridiculous and futile in ways familiar to us. I guarantee that if any ten average members of the august Stage Society

8 June '11 itself were faithfully portrayed on the stage, with all their mannerisms, absurdities and futilities, the resulting picture would be damned as a gross and offensive caricature. People never look properly at people; people take people for granted; they remain blind to the facts; and when an artist comes along and discloses more of these facts than it is usual to disclose, of course there is a row. This row is a fine thing; it means that something has been done. And I hope that the directors of the Stage Society are proud of the reception of "The Cherry Orchard." They ought to be.

SEA AND SLAUGHTER

RECENT spectacular events at Court have been the cause of a considerable amount of verse, indifferent or offensive. But it is to be noticed that the poets of this realm have not been inspired by the said events. I mean such writers as W. B. Yeats, Robert Bridges, Lord Alfred Douglas, W. H. Davies. And yet I see no reason why a Coronation, even in this day of figure-heads and revolting snobbery, should not be the subject of a good poem—a poem which would not be afflicting to read, either for the lettered public or for the chief actor in the scene. However, the time for such poems has apparently not yet arrived. And meanwhile the sea-and-slaughter school have been doing an excellent work these last few weeks in demonstrating how entirely absurd the sea-and-slaughter school is. Mr. Alfred Noyes has been very prominent, not only in his native page, *Blackwood's,* but also in the *Fortnightly Review.* Mr. Noyes is, I believe, the only living versifier whose books are, in the words of an American editor, "a commercial proposition." He is by many thought to be a poet. Personally, I have always classed him with Alfred Austin, not *6 July '11*

6 July '11 yet having come across one single stanza of his which would fall within my definition of poetry. Here is an extract from his "A Salute from the Fleet":—

Mother, O grey sea-mother, thine is the crowning cry—

I am bound to interrupt the quotation here in order to vent my feelings of extreme irritation caused by the mere phrase, "O grey sea-mother." Why should this phrase drive me to fury? It does. Well, to recommence:—

Mother, O grey sea-mother, thine is the crowning cry!
Thine the glory for ever in the nation born of thy womb!
Thine is the Sword and the Shield and the shout that Salamis heard,
Surging in Æschylean splendour, earth-shaking acclaim!
Ocean-mother of England, thine is the throne of her fame!

Fancy standing on the shore to-day and addressing the real sea in these words and accents! Fancy the poet doing it! The mood and the mentality are prehistoric. I would not mind Mr. Noyes putting himself lyrically into the woaded skin of our ancestors. But I do think he might have got a little nearer the mark in indicating the "throne of her fame." Because I expect Mr. Noyes knows as well as anybody that the real throne of England's fame is not in the sea at all. England's true fame springs from the few acts of national justice which she has accomplished, and from the generous impulses which as a nation she has had—as, for example, in her relations with Italy; as, for example, in the Factory Acts which prevented children from working eighteen hours a day six or seven days a week. The patriotic versifiers of this country will, if they persist, end by making the sea impossible for a plain man to sail on. I have long felt that I want never again to read anything about the sea except the advertisements of auxiliary yawls and cutters in the *Yachting World*. I recommend these advertisements as a balm for sores caused by rhymed marine Jingoism. *6 July '11*

A BOOK IN A RAILWAY ACCIDENT

20 July '11

BOOKS are undoubtedly cursed, and rendered unreadable in a new sense. I don't know how many years it is since I was informed that Villiers de L'Isle Adam's "L'Eve Future" was a really fine novel. I bought it, and I was so upset, in my narrow youthfulness, to find that the author had made a hero of Thomas Alva Edison, and called him by his name, that I could not accomplish more than two chapters. Later I was again informed that "L'Eve Future" was a really fine novel, and I had another brief tussle with it, and was vanquished by its dulness. I received a third warning, and started yet again, and disliked the book rather less, and then I completely lost it in a removal. After months or years it mysteriously turned up, like a fox-terrier who has run off on an errand of his own. But I did not resume it. And then after another long interval the idea that I absolutely must read "L'Eve Future" gathered force in my mind, and I decided that the next time I went away for a week-end I would take it with me. This was in France. I took it away with me. I read a hundred pages on the outward journey and I got on terms with "L'Eve Future." *"Ce livre m'attendait,"* as a certain French novelist said when he read "Tom Jones." On the return journey I was deep buried in "L'Eve Future," when a fearful jolting suddenly began to rock the saloon carriage in which I was. The jolting grew worse, very much worse. Women screamed. I saw my stick fly out of the rack above my head across the carriage. The door leading to the corridor jumped off its hinges. Then shattered glass fell in showers, and I saw an old lady beneath an arm-chair and a table. The shape of the carriage altered. And then, after an enormous crash, equilibrium was established amid the cries of human anguish. I had clung to the arms of my seat and was unhurt, but there were four wounded in the carriage. My eye-glasses were still sticking on my nose. Saying to myself that I must keep calm, I put them carefully away, and began to help to get people out of the wreck. It was not until I looked about for my belongings that I saw that the corner of a tender had poked itself into our carriage. Outside a mail-van and two enormous coaches were lying very impressively on their sides, and two wounded girls were *20 July '11*

20 July '11 lying on the grass by the track, and people were shouting for doctors. I ultimately got away with my bag and stick and hat, and walked to the nearest station, where a porter naturally asked me for my ticket. I hired an auto and reached Paris only a quarter of an hour late for dinner. And I congratulated myself on my calmness and perfect presence of mind in a railway accident. Only "L'Eve Future" was not in my bag. I had forgotten it, and my presence of mind had thus been imperfect. I did not buy another copy of "L'Eve Future," and I don't think I ever shall, now.

"FICTION" AND "LITERATURE"

PUBLISHERS' advertisements of imaginative work are so constantly curious that one gets accustomed to their bizarre qualities and refrains from comment. But Messrs. Hutchinson, who are evidently rather proud of having secured Lucas Malet's new long novel, have thought of a new adjective, and the event must be chronicled. They are announcing to the world that Lucas Malet's new novel is "literary"—"the literary novel of the autumn." I cannot be quite sure what this means, but it is probably intended to signify that, in the opinion of Messrs. Hutchinson, Lucas Malet's novel is very special—that is to say, it is not a mere novel. Less adroit publishers than Messrs. Hutchinsons might have described it as an "art novel." (*Cf.* "art furniture," all up Tottenham Court Road.) Some of the most esteemed provincial dailies have a column headed "Literature" on five days of the week, but on the sixth day that column is headed "New Fiction." You see the distinction. Messrs. Hutchinsons are doubtless hinting to the provinces that the new book is something between "literature" and "fiction," and *31 Aug. '11*

31 Aug. '11 combines the superior attributes of both. Once the *Athenæum,* apparently staggered by the discovery that Joseph Conrad existed, reviewed a novel of his under the rubric of "Literature," instead of with other novels under the rubric of fiction. Messrs. Hutchinson have possibly an eye also on the *Athenæum*. Personally, I would not permit my publishers to advertise a novel of mine as literary. But on the whole I wouldn't seriously object to the adjective "un-literary."

INDEX

INDEX

INDEX

INDEX

INDEX

www.ingramcontent.com/pod-product-compliance
Lightning Source LLC
Chambersburg PA
CBHW021215090426
42740CB00006B/234
* 9 7 8 1 4 3 4 4 2 2 1 7 0 *